Asleep with One Eye Open

Dale S. Ailes

This is a work of fiction. Names, characters, businesses, places, events and incidents are either the products of the author's imagination or used in a fictitious manner. Any resemblance to actual persons, living or dead, or actual events is purely coincidental.

Copyright © 2013 Dale S. Ailes
All rights reserved.
ISBN: **1484928040**
ISBN-13: **978-1484928042**

DEDICATION

This book is dedicated to all the teachers that take the time to not only educate the children in the classroom, but also make the effort to ensure that their students become productive citizens. This book is also dedicated to every teacher that has the courage to not only identify possible abuse in a child, but also has the courage to take a stand.

CONTENTS

	Acknowledgments	i
1	Thank a Teacher	1
2	Looking Back	9
3	On Her Own	20
4	Munchausen	29
5	The Allergy	38
6	Introducing Zander	46
7	Time for School	56
8	Dodgeball	69
9	Suspected	79
10	The Visit	91
11	A New School	103
12	Saved	114
13	The Aftermath	125
14	Back to Reality	135
	From the Author	143
	No World around Me	146

ACKNOWLEDGMENTS

I would like to thank my wife, Amy, and my daughter, Taylor for all the love and support I have received through my first writing experience.

1 THANK A TEACHER

Autumns in Northwest Indiana bring a time of change; the red, orange, yellow and brown leaves bring a beauty like no other across the region. Change is inevitable; seasons change, days change, time change, and even people change. That is no exception when it comes to one boy that is a fourth grade student at Dunes Acres Elementary School in Portage, Indiana.

Mr. Madison is meeting this morning before the start of another fine school day at this five star school that lies along the shores of Lake Michigan with Principal Taylor, and Rob Lawson, a representative from Child Services. This is a closed door meeting to discuss the next steps in the matter of removing, in actuality saving, one of the students in Mr. Madison's class from the horror this child has survived through the past ten years of his life.

What was the horror that this child endured over the ten years of his life. It has been for the most part ten years of hell: full of daily emotional and physical abuse. A home in which new and clean clothes are a luxury; a home where a month's worth of food is the same as what a normal person would eat in a day; a home that does not give this child a name or his own identity; a home that does not love him.

After about an hour of intense discussion on this horrific situation, the meeting ended; with enough time for Mr. Madison to return to his classroom and get prepared for the school day. After the meeting, Rob left with the full intention of removing this child from the home immediately, and the mother that devoted her life to the pain and suffering of her only child is getting a one way ticket to prison. As of this day, the hell has ended, and a child is free.

Monday mornings are the beginning of a new week and new lessons. This happens to be the second Monday in October. Mr. Madison's daily agenda completely revolves around Christopher Columbus. In reading, the students will be reading a Columbus play with assigned roles. Mr. Madison is combining language arts with social studies by having his students look for corrections by looking at sentences on the life and adventures of

Columbus. In math, the assignment is eight problems that all have the same answer: 1492.

At the beginning of the school day, the children stand and recite the pledge of allegiance, make their choice for lunch, and start their morning bell work. Afterwards, Principal Taylor recites the morning announcements, and then greets all students to have a wonderful Columbus Day.

While all of that is going on, Mr. Madison takes attendance. There is only one open desk in the class; the desk that belongs to the boy that he just had a meeting about earlier. Perfect attendance in the class has not been met for the first time this school year.

Throughout the announcements, Mr. Madison starts to realize the irony. A child, a student in his class, is leaving his home and put into a foster home. This will be a new adventure where nothing from this point on will ever be the same. This child has endured so many struggles and survived; just as Columbus had endured many struggles on his way to discovering America. After the discovery of America, it opened the world wide for the vast discovery and exploration of the new world. This child is just like Columbus; a new life is what this child is about to discover. That life, throughout all of the struggles, will never again be the same.

The day ends the same way every day in Mr. Madison class. Mr. Madison dedicates the last hour to one on one help with students in need while the other students work quietly in order to complete daily assignments, or they have time for free reading; in which the student has the choice on what they read. It could be a novel, a magazine, a newspaper or even a comic book; as long as they are reading, Mr. Madison is happy.

Ten minutes before the dismissal time, Mr. Madison has a group at a time collect their coats and backpacks from the closet. He makes sure that the students have any assignments not finished in their homework folders; and that all of the students' mailboxes are empty. After that, he lines the students up in front of the class and waits for the bell to ring to dismiss them. As the bell rings ending the school day, he gives every student a high five as they walk out the door.

After the students leave for the day, Mr. Madison sits down and collects himself for only a minute since every minute counts when it comes to teaching. He collects the assignments that are in the homework trays and puts them in his bag to take them home so he can grade them at home; a teacher's job never stops. He sits back down at his desk and starts organizing his materials for Tuesday when a visitor walks in his classroom. It is Principal Taylor.

"Hello Mr. Madison," Principal Taylor says.

"Hello back to you."

"Hello back to you" is like a catch-phrase for Mr. Madison. Every one of his students always greets him with a "hello", and he responds with a goofy smile and a silly voice, "Hello back to you."

"How did your day go?" Principal Taylor asks.

"The school day went superbly. I love Columbus Day," replies Mr. Madison.

"That is great to hear." Principal Taylor says. "After you had left the meeting this morning, I talked to Rob from Child Services. He informed me that the police are heading over to remove the child from that home effective immediately."

"That is the best news I have heard all day." says Mr. Madison.

"And furthermore, I just received word that the child has just been removed and placed into a foster home." Principal Taylor added. "Also, the school district has agreed to bus the student from the foster home to our school so he can remain in your class. I truly believe this would be in the best interest of the child."

"Okay, I lied, that is the best news I have heard all day......unless there is a three times a charm coming," jokes Mr. Madison.

There is a three times a charm," says Principal Taylor.

"What's that?" asks Mr. Madison.

"There are fresh baked snickerdoodles in the teachers' lounge," Principal Taylor says.

"Yippee, snickerdoodles!" exclaims Mr. Madison.

Principal Taylor and Mr. Madison head down to the teachers' lounge just in a nick of time to get some of those fresh baked snickerdoodles. When there is fresh baked anything in the teachers' lounge, things do not remain long because teachers are like vultures when they get a whiff of something baked and put on a plate.

While scrounging down the cookies, the conversation continues.

"Mr. Madison, I appreciate everything you do for our school, you have won several teaching awards, every parent lines up at my door to insist that their child is in your class. What you did for this child in my eyes in the best thing you did in your fourteen years as a teacher, and I am proud not only to have you as a dedicated colleague but also as a courageous man that took the time to educate himself to identify the signs of abuse in a child. I reward you for your efforts."

"I appreciate your kind words and your vote of confidence."

"While it will be a tough time of adjustment for this child, I know in time that everything will turn out well. I have faith in you and I will be here for you if you need me for anything in order for this child to adjust to his new settings," Principal Taylor says.

"I am so fortunate to be able to work at a school that has such a strong support cast. It reminds me of this cookie. In order for a cookie to be this good, it needs to have all of the ingredients come together and mix well. This school is like a cookie…..we all come together and support each other." Mr. Madison says. "That's what makes this school so good."

Principal Taylor agrees and says goodbye for the day. Mr. Madison returns to his classroom so he can continue his planning for the next day. When he gets to his classroom, he walks in and sits at his desk. As he sits there, he starts reflecting on the child.

"I know everything is going to be okay from this point on," he thinks to himself. "I know that when he sits there at his desk and looks at me, he realizes that what I have done for him with be life changing. From this point on, he realizes that no matter how severe things may be, or what he will go through, he knows that I will be there for him, through thick and thin."

Child abuse is such a touchy subject; it is not like reading or math. It is not something that we teach because most children do not realize that it could be happening to one of their classmates. Children that live through abuse learn not to trust adults. Most times than not, even though it could be the worst thing in the world, children that live in an abusive home are too afraid to tell anyone. Could it be that they are afraid that no one would believe them? Could it be that they are afraid the abuse might get worse? Every child abuse case is different; it all depends on the home and the problems within the home.

As Mr. Madison reflects on this situation more, he thinks to himself, "I can only imagine how rough it was at that home........."

2 LOOKING BACK

Senior year is the greatest school year in almost every teenager's lives. Seniors know that they are the top of the food chain in school. Every special occasion in school is so memorable because it will be the last one: the last homecoming, the last game, the last social gathering, the last prom. Every story they tell in the future will be those memories of senior year.

Jackson and Jennette are two seniors at Hawthorne High School in Hawthorne, Michigan living each day of their senior year to the fullest. Jackson is the star running back for the football team; already accepting a full ride scholarship to a major university. Jennette is a varsity cheerleader, and president of the student council. Both are honor students. Jennette has several college acceptance letters and is weighing her options.

Jennette has just found out some outstanding news, and she heads home to share the great news with her mother, Camille.

"Mom!" yells Jennette.

"What?" Camille asks. "And when you respond can you take it down a notch."

"Okay, Jackson asked me to the senior prom."

"That is exciting news, Jennette, I knew in time someone would ask you. Jackson is a really nice boy. You will have a great time."

"Can we go look at dresses tonight?" asks Jennette. "I can't wait."

"That sounds like an excellent plan, I wanted to go to the mall tonight to get out of the house, and now we have a reason."

They head to the mall and right away, at the very first store, Jennette finds the perfect royal blue dress with silver accessories. Jennette envisions a perfect prom in her head: the dress, jewelry, the shoes, the hair, a limousine, dinner, dancing, pictures and after prom to the waterpark resort.

With the dress, jewelry and shoes bought, Jennette is three steps closer to the perfect prom night. Three weeks later, the day arrives. Jennette signs out of school early so she can have time to get her hair and nails done. Every minute Jennette is thinking to herself how perfect her senior prom is going to be. She finishes her hair and nails by three o'clock, heads home to get her dress on since Jackson is going to be at her house by four so Camille would have time to take pictures before they left for dinner.

Jackson arrives right on time. He greets Jennette with the most beautiful wrist corsage she has ever seen; a white rose with a tint of royal blue, which matches her dress exactly. Jackson did an amazing job with the flowers.

"This is going to be the perfect night," Jennette says to herself.

After posing for it seems like a million pictures that Camille insisted on taking of Jackson and Jennette, they finally leave. Jennette is escorted by Jackson out of her home and straight to the most beautiful white stretch limousine she has ever seen. Jackson and three of his football teammates chipped in on the cost of the limousine.

Jackson and Jennette leave, and it is time for the senior prom. The limousine ride around town on the way to the senior prom is amazing. After picking up the others that are sharing the limousine,

Jackson and Jennette finally arrive at the banquet hall where the senior prom is about to begin.

"Everything to this point still is perfect," Jennette thinks to herself.

While others from the school view prom as just another formal dance, Jennette still views the senior prom as the special night she has been dreaming about since the day that Jackson asked her. Dinner is amazing, the decorations at the banquet hall are spectacular, the music is so alive; Jackson and Jennette dance to every song……senior prom is perfect.

As the prom ends, the night continues. The Raging Nile Waterpark Resort is the traditional after prom for Hawthorne High School. The resort reserves four floors of rooms for the prom goers for after the prom and opens the indoor waterpark for an all-night pool party full of swimming, waterslides, music and food.

Jennette loves the waterpark. She is especially excited about all of the extreme water slides the waterpark has to offer. There is a giant funnel ride that drops straight down from about fifty feet and sends riders through the funnel up and down each side. There are two extreme indoor water coasters that extend the length of the water park. For the people that do not like the extreme thrills, there is a wave pool, and a lazy river.

Jackson and Jennette join Stephen and Jessica, the couple they are sharing a room with at the resort, for hours of nonstop fun. After a while of rotating between the numerous waterslides, Jackson and Jennette take a break.

"This is a perfect night," Jennette says. "But I think I need a break from the water."

"This night is not over just yet," says Jackson.

"What do you mean?"

"Stephen and Jessica let me know that they are going to stay at the waterpark all night because they can sleep tomorrow when they get home so we will have the room to ourselves if we want,"

After a brief pause, Jackson adds, "If you know what I mean."

Jennette knows exactly what he means and thinks to herself, "After such a perfect night, is this truly what I want? I know that prom means sex to a lot of people, but I am ready for this?"

Jennette reflects upon everything that has happened over the course of the night and comes to a decision.

"Okay Jackson, let's go back to the room. This night has been perfect. It is all because of you

Jackson, and I want to repay you for this magnificent night."

"This is going to be a night you will never forget."

Morning comes, and after a perfect ending to a perfect night, Stephen and Jessica walk into the room.

"I told you we were pulling an all-nighter; you guys should have stayed," says Stephen.

"Yeah, too bad you two wimped out," joked Jessica.

"We had our own all-nighter," Jackson says.

Jennette adds, "And our all-nighter was probably more fun than yours."

"That is your opinion," says Stephen. "It is not an obligation to have sex because it's prom. There are so many more days that I will have the opportunity for sex, and I just wanted to have fun at the waterpark; because that is what I paid for."

"That is why I love you," Jessica says.

"Right back at you girl," says Stephen

"I didn't feel obligated to have sex," says Jennette. "I just felt it was the right time and the right place for it. The night was perfect for me."

"Stephen, quit being such a girl and admit it, you wimped out and were afraid of getting rejected," Jackson jokes.

The night comes to an end, and Jackson takes Jennette home. The night ends with one last memorable kiss.

"I will talk to you later after I wake up."

"I will be waiting by the phone."

The weekend past and Jackson still have not called. Jennette sees Jackson on Monday at school.

"I waited for your call."

"You will not believe it. I slept all day and all night. I felt that it was too late to call when I woke up and then on Sunday, I had to help my dad all day."

"Well, we are talking now, so that's okay. Prom was amazing, and I am hoping that we can go out again. I really like you, and I have a lot of fun when I am with you. I could see a future with you."

"Prom was one thing. But, I am leaving right after graduation for school to start football workouts. I do not feel there will be a place for you in my future."

"I thought we were getting along great, and I thought you like me. Now I see that it was nothing more than just a booty call for you."

"Take it however you want. I am leaving soon, and I don't want to be tied down."

"I thought you were special."

"I am special, but just not the way you want me to be so deal with it!"

Jennette smacks Jackson in the face, in front of everybody in the hallway, before the start of school and storms of crying. This is the last time Jennette talks to Jackson until the night of graduation.

New beginnings only happen when there is an ending. Graduation is not the end of the journey; it is the start of another journey. Jennette has not spoken to Jackson since she slapped him in the face on the Monday morning after prom. Jennette has not told anybody, including her mother, Camille, the news she is about to tell Jackson. She is so mad at Jackson about the whole prom thing that she chooses to share the news with him on a special night as a way to payback the misery he shared with her after prom.

"Jackson, we need to talk."

"No, we do not. You were upset, and I know you will get over it."

"I don't think I will ever get over it. I'm pregnant, and it's yours."

"How dare you come to me on graduation night and say that I knocked you up! I know that I pulled out, so there is no way that I got you pregnant. You are just mad that I dissed you after prom and now you are just trying to trap me."

"But you are the only one I have been with."

"You are nothing but a slut so that baby inside of you could be any guy in this school. Everyone knows that you get around."

"That is not true."

"You just want to ride my coattails since I am going to college to be a football god!"

"I don't want to ride anything; I just want you to know so you can take care of your responsibilities."

"I am leaving and I am not taking care of a baby that is not mine. I am done with you. Don't call me or talk to me again. Go trap someone else with this nonsense."

Jackson storms off leaving Jennette standing there is a pool of her own tears. Jennette hears a voice from behind her.

"So this is how I find out?" Camille says. "I am your mother, and instead of coming to me about this, you embarrass me in front of all of these people."

"I am sorry." I wanted to tell you, but I was scared."

"We will talk when we get home."

Camille had a surprise party for Jennette after graduation. Instead, the surprise was on her. When they got home, there was a crowd of family and friends waiting for Jennette.

"Let's not ruin this night," Camille says. "We will talk tomorrow."

The graduation party that Camille planned was a success. There was no mention of the baby. This night was all about Jennette's graduation. The next morning was another story.

Jennette wakes up and head out to the kitchen where her mother is sitting. She sits down at the table next to her.

"Sorry, I did not mean this to happen."

"You are the dumbest smart kid I know. How could you do this to me?"

"I never meant to do this to anybody, but it is what it is and I need to prepare for what is heading my way. I really need your help with this."

"I raised you to be a lot better than this. Didn't you learn anything from not having a father around all these years?"

"I made a mistake."

"You had a bright future. You were going to college. You could have made something of yourself."

"I still will go to college; I still will make something of myself. If you help me, I will be okay."

"I already raised a child on my own, and I am not raising another."

"I am not asking you to raise my baby; I just need you to be there when I need you."

"You ruined your life, and I cannot be there as a constant reminder of what you did to yourself. My life was ruined when you when born, and now it starts all over again."

"Don't say that, I did not ruin your life."

"It's time for me to live my life the way I had planned before you were born. I cannot be here for this child."

"So what are you saying?"

"I am saying that you are on your own, you will have to live your life from this point on without me. Last night you received twelve hundred dollars in graduation money and I will give you another twelve hundred. Take this money and you need to leave. I will give you a month to be gone."

Jennette takes the money and storms off crying; knowing the only person that she has relied on for so many years has turned her back on her. A month has past and Jennette is gone............living on her own for the first time in her life.

"This thing inside of me has ruined my life. I have no one now. Prom night definitely was a night I will never forget."

3 ON HER OWN

Lake Station, Indiana is a small town in the Northwest part of Indiana, approximately one hundred and sixty miles from Hawthorne, Michigan, and the now home to Jennette and a newborn boy named Zander. It is not the desired place or town to live for Jennette, but it is far enough away from everybody that turned their back on her.

Months after Camille bid a fond farewell to her only daughter; Jennette has found a cheap trailer to rent on the north side of the town.

The trailer is the cheapest place she could find, since having very little money and no support from anybody. She did have a roof over her head, and two bedrooms; one for her and one for Zander.

The only work she could find is a minimum wage job at a fast food restaurant; most of which goes to daycare while she works and the rest goes to the rent, electricity and water bills.

She can't afford much food on her own, but she does receive food stamps but not much. Most of the food stamps go to buying formula for Zander. Most of Jennette's food comes from the restaurant she worked at. When she does have a little extra money, which is rare, she uses it to buy extra diapers and a bottle of whiskey, which at this time, seems to be her only friend.

Jennette does not have any friends and can never afford to go out to the movies or even the mall. She has a hard time going to the mall because it depresses her so much that she is not able to buy anything.

She does have a car that she bought with the money from graduation. She took one thousand of those dollars and bought a cheap used car. She can barely afford gas, so she only drives to the daycare center and back. She walks to work which is about a mile away.

When she is not working, Jennette is at home, with Zander. "Is this the future I envisioned when she was a month away from graduation? Did I deserve to live her life this way? Why does nobody care about me?" Jennette says to herself.

These are the questions that are going through her mind while trying to watch television on one of the few channels she is able to get through the use of rabbit ears; while drinking whiskey straight from the bottle. But, like every single moment of every single day, her peace and quiet is interrupted by a loud cry.

"Why don't you ever sleep?" screams Jennette. "I am so tired and need some time for myself. You don't deserve my attention. I just want this thing to leave me alone!"

While Zander is the name given to the child at birth, Jennette never calls him by name. She just calls him "this thing or that thing".

"All you do is cry, poop and eat. I wish you would just sleep."

At that moment, Jennette came up with an idea. Jennette makes a bottle of formula but adds a shot of whiskey from the bottle that she was consuming earlier.

"This thing will sleep now."

Jennette feeds to bottle to Zander, and he falls fast asleep. Zander actually sleeps for eight straight hours for the first straight time since he was born.

"I wish I would think of this earlier."

This became an everyday event for Jennette. Every time Zander wakes up, Jennette would add a shot of whiskey to the bottle and Zander would go fast asleep and stay asleep all of the time.

The only problem that Jennette sees in her plan is that she would have to buy more whiskey in order to keep Zander asleep more hours so she could have time for herself. She either needed to find a way to make more money or sacrifice something to free up the money to buy more whiskey because she is now sharing it with Zander.

One night while finishing off her own bottle of whiskey, Jennette comes up with a solution to get the money to pay for the whiskey.

"Does that thing really need diapers?" Jennette says to herself. "Diapers are such a waste of money."

Jennette stop buying diapers immediately. Walking on her way home from work, but before she picked up Zander at daycare, Jennette found a pile of newspapers sitting in a dumpster.

"I will just line the crib with newspaper so if that thing goes, the newspaper will soak it up. I will just save the diapers for the daycare."

Jennette arrives at home, and immediately strips the crib bedding off, and covers the entire crib with newspaper.

"If that thing goes poop or pee, I will just take the top layer of newspaper off, and the fresh ones will be under it, problem solved."

"No more diaper changing for me."

Jennette picks up Zander from daycare and takes him home. She immediately feeds one of her special whiskey bottles to Zander, and he falls fast asleep. Jennette removes his clothes and lays him in the crib naked on top of the newspaper.

"Finally, I will have time to myself: no more changing diapers and this thing will sleep all of the time," Jennette says old loud. "Finally, I might be able to have my own life without that thing." Jennette kicks back a tall glass of whiskey for herself and sleeps the night away, just as Zander now has been doing for months.

The next morning, Jennette wakes up to a crying Zander. Since Jennette has to work early, Zander will have to spend the morning at daycare. Jennette goes into Zander's room, takes him out of the crib and tosses him on the ground, like a stuffed animal, so she can change the newspaper in the crib. When she picks him back up, she notices a red mark on Zander's head.

"Great job Jennette," she says to herself. "That stupid thing has a mark on his head. And he has to go to daycare soon."

She gets Zander dressed, puts a diaper on him (the only time he ever has a diaper on), fills two bottles with nonalcoholic formula and takes Zander to daycare. When she arrives at the daycare center leader, Crissa Walters greets her.

"Good morning, Jennette," Crissa says.

"Hello, Crissa."

"What happened to Zander? He has a huge red mark on his head."

"Zander woke up last night for a bottle so I took him into the bedroom with me and I must have dozed off and he accidentally rolled off the bed. I felt so horrible."

"That seems kind of strange."

"Why does that seem strange to you?"

"When Zander is here, he barely moves around; and he has never rolled over. Are you sure that is what happened?"

"Of course that is what happened," yells Jennette. "I already feel horrible about this, and I know I need to watch him more carefully when he is in bed with me."

"Well, if that is the story you are sticking with, I guess I believe you. But, you should invest in rails for your bed or prop pillows up to block him from rolling off."

"Thanks, I will do that."

As Jennette leaves the daycare center, she thinks to herself, "How dare Crissa accuse me of something I did not do to that thing."

"But Crissa does make a good point," she thinks to herself. "That thing is not getting any bigger, that thing is not making any sounds other than cries, and that thing is not even crawling yet."

This was a rare day since Jennette chose to drive to work. But there was a reason for this. On her lunch break, she heads back to her trailer and removes the crib from Zander's room and covers the floor completely with newspaper.

"Now he has more room to move around; maybe that stupid thing will figure out how to crawl on his own. If that thing wants out of its room, that thing will have to move."

Jennette lays Zander down on the floor in his makeshift bedroom on top of the newspaper and gives him one of the special whiskey laced bottles. Zander falls fast asleep for the night.

"I need to do something," Jennette thinks out loud, "This thing will ruin my life even more if it does not start to move around……and grow."

The next morning Jennette puts an end to the whiskey laced bottles, and starts giving Zander bottles of whole milk. Jennette feeds him constantly, and it starts to show…..Zander is beginning to grow.

"Now that this thing is beginning to grow, it needs to start moving around."

Saturday is Jennette's day off. She notices the yard sale down the street. Jennette walks down the street and finds the answer to her problems………a baby walker.

"How much for the walker," Jennette asks the woman at the yard sale.

"I am selling it for ten dollars," the woman says.

"I only have five dollars; would you take five dollars for it?"

"Five dollars will be fine."

Jennette gives the woman five dollars and carries the walker back to her trailer and immediately puts Zander into the walker.

"This should put an end to that thing's not moving around. I will just leave it in there all of the time."

Jennette does leave him in their all of the time. Zander even sleeps in an upright position. In time, Zander figures out for himself how to move around.

"Two problems solved. Now all this thing needs to do is learn how to talk. But I am not talking to that thing."

The days of Zander sleeping on top of newspaper in his bedroom are over; the days of sleeping in his walker have begun. Zander now sleeps in the living room with the television on at all times.

"The TV will teach this thing how to speak. If this doesn't work, I will just have to take it to the doctor."

A few months have passed since Jennette has kept Zander in the walker, and it is starting to pay off. He is starting to move around as if he is a normal child. But, with Jennette failing to talk to Zander on a normal basis, Zander is still not talking.

"Well, I am not going to be accused of doing something wrong again by that little tramp Crissa that thinks she knows how tough it is for me and has the gall to accuse me of hurting my own child."

4 MUNCHAUSEN

The Northern Indiana Health Clinic is a publicly funded medical center for those that have financial need like that of Jennette's situation. The clinic provides next to nothing medical care for low income families. The clinic is open on a walk-in basis. Jennette takes Zander to the clinic.

"I think something is wrong with my child."

"What seems to be the problem?" the nurse at the counter asks.

"Well, my child Zander is almost one year old, and he is just starting to grow, and he is not talking at all."

"Okay, we will let the doctor take a look at him."

After waiting what it seems like a lifetime in the waiting room, Jennette finally goes back with Zander to see the doctor. After a few minutes, Dr. Rustin walks in the room.

"Hello, what seems to be the problem?"

"My son, Zander, is almost one year old and still is not talking. Am I doing something wrong?"

"Well, Jennette, this is a common thing in children. Don't feel like you are at fault here. Babies tend to start talking in their own time. But, let's examine him to make sure everything is okay."

Dr. Rustin examines Zander thoroughly. He checks Zander breathing, his ears, his eyes, his reflexes, and he even checks his weight. While examining Zander, he even gets Zander to smile; for the very first time.

"The only thing I see is that Zander is just a little underweight. A lot of time young mothers tend to keep their babies on formula too long. You need to start giving Zander real food now, and he should be a good size in no time. As for Zander not talking, the best advice I can give you is talk to him on a normal basis and even try reading stories to him. The more he hears, the more he will try to repeat."

Jennette leaves with Zander feeling good knowing that a doctor has told her that she is doing nothing wrong.

"A doctor knows more than the stupid bitch Crissa."

A couple of weeks later, Jennette returns to the clinic with Zander.

"Hello Jennette," says the nurse behind the counter. "What seems to be the problem with Zander?"

"I have been feeding him baby food the past couple of weeks and every time I feed him, he throws up."

"Go ahead and take him straight back, the doctor is ready for him."

"Hello, Jennette," says Dr. Rustin. "How is Zander doing?"

"He is having trouble keeping the baby food down. As soon as his eats it, he is puking it right back up."

"This is common for babies, Jennette. Babies spit up when they eat. That does not mean that Zander is sick. Maybe he just does not like the food you are giving him. Try feeding him a different brand of baby food. I am sure that will make a difference."

Two weeks later, Jennette is back at the clinic with Zander.

"Zander has been coughing, sneezing, and his nose is running. He has been running a fever."

"Let me take a look," says Dr. Rustin.

After examining Zander for a brief period, Dr. Rustin talks to Jennette.

"I have looked Zander over, and he seems to be fine. He has no temperature, and he hasn't coughed a single time since he has been here."

"What are you saying?"

"Are you sure this is not just an attempt to get attention?"

"How dare you say that? I am worried that something is wrong with my son, and you are talking to me like I am a basket case," screams Jennette.

Jennette leaves the clinic annoyed.

"I can't believe that useless doctor did not even do anything. The next time I will make sure that Dr. Rustin knows something is wrong."

After Jennette leaves Dr. Rustin heads to the office down the hall. This office belongs to Dr. Harrison, the psychologist that volunteers at the clinic.

"Dr. Harrison, do you have a minute?"

"What can I help you with?"

"I have a patient that has brought her son to the clinic on numerous occasions the past few weeks. Every time, I find nothing wrong with her son."

"So if there is nothing wrong, why are you coming to me about this?"

"I am just getting a real bad vibe about this situation. It seems like the mother is looking for attention and I just have a weird feeling she might do something to hurt her son."

Dr. Harrison thinks for a minute.

"You need to make a record of every doctor visit, and we will go from there. If your weird vibe is right, she will be back in a couple of weeks. When that happens I will sit in on the appointment."

"I will let you know if she returns."

Two weeks have passed, and Jennette has not yet returned to the clinic. But at the beginning of the third week, Jennette returns with Zander.

"Hello, Jennette," says the nurse at the counter.

"Hello, Zander seems to have trouble breathing. I am worried that he might be getting asthma."

"Okay, I will take you right back. The doctor will be right in."

A few minutes go by when Jennette is greeted by Dr. Rustin. Dr. Harrison is with him.

"Welcome back Jennette," says Dr. Rustin. "This is Dr. Harrison. He will be sitting in on the examination. What seems to be the problem?"

"Zander seems to be having trouble breathing," says Jennette.

"Let me check him."

Dr. Rustin checks Zander's breathing.

"He seems to be breathing just fine."

"Oh thank God. I truly thought there was something wrong this time."

"He is as fit as a fiddle,"

"Thank you for checking him out."

"You are very welcome, Jennette."

"Okay, I will see you next time."

"Before you go, Jennette, Dr. Harrison is wondering if you would want to talk before you leave. He is our resident psychologist."

"What the hell is this?" screams Jennette.

"I am hoping to talk to you about your situation," Dr. Harrison says.

"And what situation would that be?"

"Dr. Rustin and I just want to discuss the reasoning behind bringing Zander to the clinic so many times lately when it is obvious that there is nothing wrong with him."

"I don't have time for this. And how dare you accuse me of anything? If you want to accuse me of anything, accuse me of caring too much about my child."

"I am not accusing you of anything Jennette. I just thought you would like to talk. I am a great listener."

"And again, I don't have time for this, and I don't have time for you."

Jennette leaves the clinic extremely upset.

"This is the very last time I come to this clinic. Did those two idiot doctors get their licenses from the back of a cereal box?"

Jennette heads home with Zander. When she walks in the door, she tosses him on the ground and heads back to the laundry room.

"I cannot believe this thing and those doctors are trying to ruin my life."

Out of anger, Jennette swings towards the closest thing she can hit. She punches the bottle of bleach right off the counter next to the washer. The bleach bottle hits the ground and the cap breaks off, leaving a pool of bleach on the floor.

"What else can go wrong today? Screw it, I am done, I am not cleaning that up, it can stay there for all I care."

Jennette leaves the laundry room and sits on the couch thinking about the doctor visit.

"I need to find a new doctor's office because I am not going back to the clinic. Those doctors are mental, and I don't want that thing around them."

Jennette looks around and notices that Zander is not where she left him.

"Where did that stupid thing go?"

Jennette goes down the hall and finds Zander in the laundry room playing in the pool of bleach that she left on the floor.

"You stupid little thing!"

Jennette kicks Zander away from the bleach on the ground, and he hits his head on the side of the dryer. Zander starts crying.

"Great, not only you are so stupid that you play in bleach, but also I now have to hear you cry about it."

Jennette grabs Zander by the arm and tosses him into his room and shuts the door. Zander cries at the door.

"You can cry all you want but you are in there for the night so you might and well go to sleep."

After about a half an hour of crying, Zander falls asleep. Jennette eats dinner, followed by several full glasses of whiskey and heads to bed.

The next morning, Jennette wakes up and gets ready for work. She walks in to where Zander is to wake him up for daycare and finds something truly wrong……Zander has a huge rash on both arms.

5 THE ALLERGY

"Oh, that is just great! This stupid thing really needs to go to the doctor now............and there is no way I am taking this thing back to the clinic so I can have two uneducated doctors accuse me of hurting my own child. That is so unprofessional. I guess I will just have to find another doctor's office to take this thing to have this rash checked out. I can't believe this stupid thing is going to cost me money because I now have to call off work."

Jennette looks in the phone book for clinics that are close to her home. She finds a clinic for low income families in the next town over, Portage, Indiana. It is next door to Portage High School which is only a couple of miles from Jennette's trailer.

Jennette drives Zander to the new clinic and is greeted the same way she was greeted at the last clinic.

"Hello," says the nurse behind the counter, "how may I help you?"

"This is my son, Zander. When I woke him up he had this huge rash over both of his arms."

"Did he come in contact with anything that might have caused the rash?"

"I knocked over a bottle of bleach last night, and it spilled all over the place. He may have come in contact with some of it while I was cleaning it up. He was crawling around while I was cleaning it."

"Oh, accidents happen. We will take good care of Zander. Is this your first time here?"

"This is my first time taking him anywhere."

"Okay, you need to fill out some paperwork, but, with the severity of the rash, we will take Zander straight back, and you can fill out the paperwork while waiting for the doctor."

Jennette nervously takes Zander back to the examination room. The doctor walks in the room.

"Hello, I am Dr. Walters; I see that somebody has got into something he should have."

"I'm Jennette, and this is Zander, and it was an accident."

"I understand, but accident or not, this might have been a good thing."

"How can a rash be a good thing?" Jennette reluctantly replies.

"Zander might have an allergy to what he came in contact with. But we need to do tests to find out exactly."

With a very relieved look, Jennette replies, "okay."

Dr. Walters runs tests on Zander and treats his rashes with an ointment. He leaves the room for what seems to be a lifetime.

The wait is a real stressing situation for Jennette after the past experiences at the other clinic. Is the doctor back talking to a psychologist? Does the doctor believe her story? Is Jennette in serious trouble?

Jennette decides the wait is not worth it. She grabs the tube of cream and places it in her coat and prepares to walk out with Zander. But, it's too late. As she is ready to leave the room, Dr. Walters walks in.

"Are you going somewhere?"

"Oh, I need to go to the bathroom."

"Okay, two doors down on the left. I will stay here with Zander until you get back."

Jennette walks out of the room with a scared look on her face. The good thing is that she is heading to the bathroom. The nervousness in her stomach makes her feel as she has to vomit. She takes a few minutes to collect herself in the bathroom before returning to the examination room.

"Good, you're back. Zander is going to be fine. The rash will go away in time with medication."

Jennette gets the feeling as if a ton of bricks has been lifted off of her shoulders.

"That's great news."

"But….," Dr. Walters adds.

"But what," Jennette says nervously.

"The chlorine in the bleach is what caused Zander's rash. He has an allergy to chlorine. This medicated cream will help clear the rash up quicker."

"That will be super," Jennette says in relief.

"For now, it would be best that you do not use bleach in your laundry and avoid any cleaners that use chlorine. I can provide a list of household products I recommend. But, get any products out of your home that contains chlorine so another accident won't happen. But by chance another accident does, don't be afraid to bring Zander back; I will help you take care of it."

"Thank you so much Dr. Walters, you are the best."

Jennette leaves the clinic thinking, "Wow, see, Dr. Rustin truly is an idiot. Dr. Walters has it going on."

Jennette leaves and takes Zander home. When she walks in the door, Jennette starts collecting all of the cleaners that contain chlorine and puts them in a box to throw in the dumpster. Jennette hesitates and looks into the box and starts to get annoyed.

"Do you know how much money I spent on this stuff and how much I am going to have to spend to replace all of this stuff?"

Jennette pauses and then screams at Zander, "you stupid thing, do you know how much this stuff cost me. What can't you be normal? You know what; I am not throwing any of this away. A rash won't kill you. I am keeping all of this, and I will use it. I don't care if it makes you sick."

Jennette unpacks the box and puts all of the cleaners back into the storage area. Afterwards, she takes a bowl of cereal and puts it in Zander's room. Then, she puts Zander in the room and closes the door.

"There, you have food and then go to bed. I am going out because I have to get you stupid medicine so that bitch Crissa won't say I hurt you on purpose again."

Jennette already has the ointment; Dr. Walters gave it to her. She leaves and heads to the bar instead.

A few weeks later, Zander breaks out in the rash again. Jennette returns with Zander to Dr. Walter's clinic.

"Zander broke out in the rash again. But I don't know how it happened. I took all the products that have bleach or chlorine out of the house and switched to organic cleaners."

"That is great that you switched." But, is there anywhere Zander might be going that he might come in contact with chlorine?"

"He does go to daycare."

"What you need to do the next time you drop Zander off is let the people at the daycare know about the allergy, I will give you paperwork you can give them. They are required, by law, to remove chlorinated products from the center if they are informed of a child having a chlorine allergy by a doctor."

Dr. Walters applies more cream to the rash and sends Jennette on her way but not before giving her a prescription for Zander.

"I put more ointment on Zander's rash. I will give you the rest of the tube. Apply it twice a day and please keep it cleaned and covered."

"I will I promise. I will take great care of him."

"Also, this prescription is for when Zander goes to the daycare. Give Zander fifty milliliters once each day he goes to daycare. It should help if he comes in contact with anything while there."

Jennette says goodbye to Dr. Walters and leaves the clinic in a very bad mood.

"I cannot believe that Crissa accused me of deliberately hurting my child, and now she is why this thing is getting rashes. I could kill her."

Jennette heads home and immediately puts Zander in his room with a bowl of cereal and closes the door. Jennette walks to the pharmacy down the street. Jennette walks to the counter and hands the pharmacist the prescription.

"This will take a couple of hours; I don't have the medicine in stock right now, but our other store has it. I can drive to get it. If you come back in a couple of hours, it will be ready."

"Before you go, how much is it going to cost?" asks Jennette.

"It depends on your insurance coverage."

"I don't have insurance."

"Without insurance, you are looking at about one hundred and twenty dollars."

"Okay, I will be back later to pick it up."

Jennette leaves and never returns to pick up the medication. Instead, she walks even further down the street to the bar on the corner. After a few drinks, Jennette heads back home. She walks in an opens the door to Zander's room; Zander is asleep on the floor. She turns the light off and closes the door.

"There is no way I am spending this much money on this thing. I already lost a whole days pay. I am so sick of this thing ruining my life. I am going to make that thing pay for what he has done to me. It will regret ever being born."

6 INTRODUCING ZANDER

"Mommy"

"What are you doing out of your room? I told you to stay in there, and I don't want to see your ugly face ever."

"But....but, I am hungry."

"See, you are such a stupid thing, you can't even talk right. I put a bowl of cereal in your room. So eat that."

"It's all gone, and I am still hungry."

"Too bad, you are not getting anything else until tomorrow. You should have thought about that before eating it so quick. Now get back in your room."

"Pease, mommy, let me sit by you."

"No, you are not welcome in my home…..that is your home so enjoy. I give you food daily; you have a room to sleep in. And I was even nice enough to buy a couple of toys for you at a garage sale, so you have plenty to do."

"But, I want to sit next to you."

"GET IT THROUGH YOUR THICK HEAD, I DON'T WANT YOU, I NEVER DID, AND IF I WOULDN'T GET IN TROUBLE, I WILL THROW YOU IN THE GARBAGE; BECAUSE THAT IS WHAT YOU ARE……GARBAGE."

Jennette gets up, and grabs Zander by the arm and drags him back to his room.

"And don't come out again."

Jennette closes the door and locks him in from the outside.

"There, you can't get out again."

Jennette is now a manager at the fast food restaurant she started at when she first went out on her own. When she received the promotion, she let everybody know that she would be able to work any hours because Zander left to go live with her mother, Camille.

But, Zander never left, he has been living locked inside of the trailer in that one room that is his sanctuary.

Jennette stopped taking Zander to daycare; because she was tired of Crissa blaming her for intentionally hurting her child. So, when Jennette works, Zander remains at home locked inside of his room……and nobody knows he is still there.

One day when Zander is alone at the trailer, he sits in his room. All he does is play and tell stories to himself.

"I am Zander; I am five years old, maybe. I live with my mommy. My mommy doesn't play with me. All I eat is cereal. I stay in my room all of the time….unless I have to go potty. My mommy doesn't love me."

"I am so afraid of my mommy; she hurts me all of the time. She makes me cry. I always have ouchies all over. She always yells at me. I must be a bad boy because she is always mad."

"She does give me baths from time to time, but the water makes me arms and legs turn red….and it makes me sick. She tells me there is nothing she can do about it."

"I have a room to play and sleep in. I sleep on the floor with a pillow and a blanket. I have toys too. I have a handful of cars, two dinosaurs, one army guy, a small ball, and a soft elephant that I like to sleep with. I used to have a baseball bat, but my mommy took it. She likes to hit me with it when she drinks too much pop and falls on the ground and gets mad and starts yelling. Sometimes, I sneak out of my room, and I try to hide the bat, but she finds other things to hit me with…..like a belt…………..or a big wood spoon."

"I remember one time mommy would not let me out to go the bathroom. I went potty in my pants. Mommy hit me so hard all over that I could not even sit down. She did not give me anymore clothes. I stayed in them same clothes for a lot of days."

"I just want my mommy to love me. I want to play outside. I miss my friends that I play with at the place where she used to take me before she went to give people food. I hate being in this room. I wish I could watch TV. I want to watch cartoons."

"I remember getting sandwiches that had peanut butter and purple jelly on them when I was at the place with my friends. I wish mommy would make me one of those. She probably doesn't know how to make one……that is why she just gives me cereal."

Zander stops telling stories and starts playing.

"The army guy is under attack!"

"The dinosaur is going to eat him."

"The army guy is the hero! Throw the ball bomb and blow up the dinosaur."

"The army guy wins!"

"The army guy gets on his elephant and rides to fweedom!"

Zander is so into playing with his toys that he does not hear the door unlock and Jennette walk in. He hears something that he has never heard from her.

"Zander"

"Yes, mommy"

"I have a surprise for you."

"What's that?"

"I brought a kid's meal home for you. It has a cheeseburger, fries, cookies and apple juice. It even has a toy in the box....a toy robot. And, I will let you eat in the living room while you watch cartoons."

Zander is extremely happy. He runs out of his room and drops down on the floor in front of the television. He has every bit of the kid's meal completely gone within minutes.

"I have more news for you. Tomorrow I do not have to work because I start my vacation, so I thought we could go to the beach and make sand castles; it is really fun."

"I can't wait, hooray.......I love you mommy!"

"I will let you watch cartoons for a half an hour and then you will have to take a bath."

Jennette gives Zander a bath. For the first time, Zander's arms and legs do not break out.

"Mommy, you fixed the water!"

"Yes, I did."

After the bath, Jennette dresses Zander in new pajamas that she found at the thrift store.

"I bought you five new shirts and pants also, and I found a pair of shorts you can go swimming in."

"I don't know how to swim."

"I will teach you tomorrow."

Zander is happy, his mommy finally loves him. He is tired from the bath, so he falls asleep on the couch. Jennette covers him up and lets him sleep there all night.

Zander wakes up to a smell that he has never smelt before. Jennette has made pancakes and bacon. She has a plate waiting for Zander at the table. Zander eats it as if it is the last meal he will ever receive.

Jennette dresses Zander in his new shorts and a new t-shirt. The two of them head to the beach. They make sand castles, Jennette helps Zander to swim, and they even climb up and down the big hill. It is a day the Zander will never forget.

After the beach, Jennette takes Zander to the park. Jennette packs a picnic lunch for the two of them. She even made peanut butter and jelly sandwiches. After they eat, Jennette plays with Zander at the playground for hours.

After a full day of quality time, Zander is happily exhausted. Zander falls asleep in the car on the way home.

The next morning Zander wakes up on the floor covered up in the corner of his room.

"Was this just a dream?" he thought to himself.

Zander went from happy to sad within seconds. Did what went on yesterday really happen? That is when he looks down and notices that he is still wearing the t-shirt and shorts that he wore to the beach yesterday.

"Zander, breakfast is ready."

Zander walks out and finds on a plate eggs, sausage, and a piece of toast. Zander went from sad back to happy. He eats everything within minutes again.

"Let's go change your clothes. I thought we could go to the zoo today and see the animals…..all the way in Chicago!"

Zander doesn't know what Chicago is, and he does not even care.

"Is there gonna be elephants there, I love elephants."

"Yes there is, this zoo has two elephants."

Zander is so happy, he gets to go out again and spend time with his mother.

"I love you, mommy!"

The day at the zoo is so much fun. Zander sees so many animals. He sees the lions asleep on a big rock, a white bear swimming in the water, a hippo completely standing under water, and the best sight of all: elephants.

Zander even gets to ride the carousel at the zoo. It doesn't have horses, but zoo animals. He rides on a camel with Jennette's help.

Before leaving, Zander gets one more surprise, a gift shop. Jennette buys Zander a plastic tube of zoo animals and a new t-shirt with elephants on it. This is the happiest day in Zander's life.

"I love you, mommy!"

The two of them leave the zoo and start to make the long trip back to Lake Station. Zander falls asleep in the car again.

When the two of them arrived home, Zander is still asleep. Jennette unfastens his seat belt and picks him up to carry him inside. As she is taking him out of the car, Jennette hits Zander's head on the door of the car. Luckily, Zander flinches but falls back asleep.

The next morning, Jennette is sitting in the living room when Zander wakes up. He has a huge knot on his head.

"That's just great, I am trying to do the right thing, and I accidentally injure my own child. But, I can't let anybody know what I did. But, I can't take him out in public either with that bump on his head."

Jennette pauses for a brief minute and realizes she has insurance now. So she takes Zander to see Dr. Walters.

"Don't tell me, Zander has a cold and needs medicine," Dr. Walters says jokingly.

Jennette just gives him a confused look.

"Just kidding, I see the bump on his head. How did this happen?"

"We were playing hide and seek outside. I hid behind a tree and Zander came running. He tripped over a root sticking out of the ground and hit the tree."

"Common occurrence with kids, accidents happen; it is part of being a kid. Zander seems to be fine. Just apply ice to it a couple times and the bump should go down."

Jennette leaves the clinic relieved that Dr. Walters believed her story, but she is upset that it looks as she is abusing her child.

Jennette drives home, not before getting them pizza for lunch. Jennette spends another fun filled day with Zander before putting him to bed in his room once again. As she walks out of his room, she looks back and stares at the bump on his head.

"That bump better go away quick; I don't want anybody else accusing me of anything again."

But what makes her nervous even more, Zander is starting kindergarten in a couple of weeks.

7 TIME FOR SCHOOL

"Finally, I am going to be able to have a life now that he is going to school. I can realize a life of my own."

Zander is excited; he gets to go to school. He gets to make new friends; he gets to be outside more.

The first week of school is one of the best weeks of Zander's life. Not only he is learning a lot of new things that he should have learned early in life, but also he feels safe going home knowing that his mom is not hurting him anymore.

The second week of school starts no different; Zander is learning even more and having so much fun in school. But things are about to change.

Jennette decides to go to college finally. Since Zander is in school, she signs up for online classes that enable her to work around the school schedule. Since she is a single mother, she receives full funding for her schooling.

Jennette's life is finally starting to turn for the better. She has a good job. She makes better money. She is bettering herself through education.

But, with the amount of hours that is needed between work and school, she does not have a lot of time for Zander.

"I really need help right now. I do not want to send him to after school daycare because of the nightmare Crissa caused last time, so maybe I will call my mom for help."

Jennette stands staring at the phone for the longest time trying to get the courage to call her mom. Finally, she dials the number.

"Mom"

"What do you want?"

"It has been five years, and you have not once tried to contact me."

"You never told me where you went."

"I moved to Indiana with Zander. He just turned six years old and just started school. I am working full time and just finally started college. Things are going good for me."

"That's good to hear but why did you call?"

"I want you to be a part of our lives. It would make it easier for me to take classes if I had help with Zander."

"I told you five years ago that I was done with you. My life is going great, and nothing is going to change that. You survived on your own five years, so you will be able to survive for more years to come. Don't call me again!"

Camille hangs up on her.

"I can't believe she still can be mad at me after all these years. I am her only child. What a bitch."

Jennette decides to make one more call.

"Hello, Jackson."

"Who is this?"

"It's me, Jennette."

"Jennette who?"

"You know, the mother of your child."

"I have no child with you."

"When are you going to admit that you are a father?"

"I am a father, I have a child of my own; and I am happily married."

"I thought no one was going to stop you from being a football god."

"I was a football god, and now I am a sportscaster. I married my college sweetheart right out of college. We had a child less than a year later. A child I know is mine……not like what you tried to trap me with."

"I don't want to argue with you, I just want some help….whatever you can give."

"This is about money, ain't it?"

"I don't want money; I just want you to be part of Zander's life."

"Why would I be a part of a kid's life that is not mine? You are just as mental as you were in high school. And you probably are still a big slut?"

Jennette slams the phone on Jackson and storms out of the trailer and heads straight to the bar down the street. Jennette makes it home about fifteen minutes before the bus drops Zander off at home.

When Zander arrives at home, he finds his mother awake but drunk on the couch.

"Mommy, I drew a picture for you."

Jennette grabs the picture from his hand, looks at it; and then rips it to shreds.

"Mommy, why did you do that? I made that special for you."

"Get out of my sight! Go to your room where you belong. I don't want to see you. You ruined my life."

"Can I have a snack first?"

"Did you eat lunch at school?"

"Yes, the school made sloppy…"

"I didn't ask what you ate stupid, I asked you if you ate. And since I know you did, you don't need a snack. Go to your room and I better not see your face the rest of the night."

Zander heads to his room and closes the door. He pulls out a box from his closet that has his toy zoo animals in and begins to play zoo.

Jennette flies the door open a few minutes later.

"You are making too much freaking noise, can you shut the hell up."

"Sorry, I will be quiet."

"Don't talk back to me you stupid thing," Jennette screams as she smacks him in the face.

"Go to the bathroom and then back to your room. You do not leave your room for anything. You are grounded."

Jennette goes back in the living room where she passes out on the couch moments later. Zander sneaks out of his room to check on her.

"Mommy must have drunk way too much pop again."

Zander sneaks into the kitchen and grabs a juice box and some fruit snacks and heads back to his room and he shuts the door. Zander plays with his toys the rest of the night before falling asleep on the floor.

Jennette wakes up about four in the morning and goes straight back to the bottle. After a couple of hours of drinking and watching television, she heads into Zander's room to wake him up for school.

"What the hell is this?"

She grabs Zander up off the floor and starts to shake him vigorously.

"I told you last night that you were not allowed out of your room and that you could not have a snack."

Jennette throws him on to the ground.

"What is this wrapper and juice box doing in here, you disobeyed me you stupid shit."

"I was hungry last night."

"You are so stupid, not only did not disobey me, but also you have the nerve to talk back to me."

"Mommy, please don't hurt me again, I love you, mommy."

"Well I don't love you!"

"Mommy you were drinking too much pop again."

"That is none of your business. Since you took food last night, you will get no breakfast today. Get yourself dressed, and wait outside for the bus."

The bus comes about an hour later, and Zander heads to school. As soon as he walks in the door, Zander heads straight to the cafeteria.

Zander reluctantly asks, "How much does that breakfast cost?"

The cafeteria worker goes to her computer and looks up Zander's profile.

"You are on free lunch, so you get breakfast free as well."

Zander is relieved, not only does he get to eat lunch at school every day, but now he gets to eat breakfast also.

But breakfast that morning is not enough to lift Zander's spirit. He finishes eating his breakfast and takes a slow walk down to the classroom. Ms. Miller greets him at the door.

"Good morning, Zander."

Zander raises his arm as to say hello but does not say a word to Ms. Miller. Instead he just walks in, grabs his morning work and sits down and starts working. As usual, the work is really hard for him, but he does not ask for help.

More of Zander's classmates come in and try to greet him, but Zander makes no response. It is as if Zander is a zombie. He sits at his desk and does not say a word the whole first part of the day.

Today is a great day for lunch. The cafeteria is making Zander's favorite lunch: grilled cheese sandwich and tater tots.

Zander grabs the tray of food and looks at it with a blank stare which is unusual knowing that his favorite meal is looking right back at him. He sits down next to a few of his classmates but does not say a word. He nibbles at his lunch but eventually eats it all.

Recess is a great time for Zander also. While a few kids like to play on the playground, the rest get to play kickball. What a way to get all of their energy out before heading back to class to finish the school day.

When Zander walks out for recess, he sits on the ground, and just watches the rest of the kids play. Despite several of his classmates asking him to play, Zander just sits there and watches the entire game.

After recess, Zander walks into the classroom and straight to his desk. He still does not talk to anyone.

Ms. Miller starts reading a story about a boy that is having a bad day……everything he does goes bad…….he has the worst luck.

Zander thinks to himself, "This Alexander kid doesn't know what a bad day is……..try coming to my house."

After Ms. Miller finishes the story, she has her students draw a picture of another way that Alexander could have had a bad day.

While the children are working, she calls Zander to her desk.

"You seem very quiet today. Is everything okay?"

"I'm fine."

"You don't seem like you are fine."

"I stayed up too late last night, and I am just a little tired."

"Well, if there is anything that is bugging you at any time, I am here for you."

"Okay, thank you. Can I go finish my picture?"

"Yes you may. But if you need help, I'm here."

Zander returns to his desk and draws a little boy in a room with no bed sitting on the floor with an unhappy look on his face.

The day ends like any other day, and Zander walks out of the classroom and straight to his bus with a very slow walk like he did not want to get on the bus.

Ms. Miller returns to her classroom and notices Zander's picture on his table. She makes an immediately phone call.

"Hello."

"Hello, this is Ms. Miller, Zander's teacher."

"What do you want?"

"I was a little concern about how Zander acted in school today. He seemed like he was out of it all day."

"I don't know what to tell you; he seemed fine when for school today."

"If there is anything you need from me, let me know."

"The one thing and only thing you can do for me is teach my child…..and don't call me every time he seems out of it."

Jennette hangs the phone up on Ms. Miller.

Zander gets off the bus ten minutes later and walks in.

"Your teacher called. She said you were bad in class today."

"I didn't do anything."

"That's right you didn't do anything, you just sat there."

"I wasn't bad."

"You were too, I paid money to send you to school and you are wasting my time and money just sitting there."

"But, I didn't get in trouble."

"You're in big trouble now."

A new night, the same story; Zander spends another extremely painful night in his room, without dinner and without love.

The next morning, Zander wakes up to a bowl of cereal in his room. Zander does not eat it. Instead, he puts the cereal in his closet and stacks his toys on top of it. He makes this a nightly ritual in case he does not get dinner.

Zander walks out of his room to a stumbling mom.

"Get dressed and go to………………….."

Zander doesn't hesitate because he hears how much his mom is struggling with her speech. He gets on the bus and heads to school and straight to breakfast. He has been eating breakfast every day at school, but his mom does not know it.

But at home, Jennette is trying to collect herself so she can go to work. She changes her clothes, brushes her teeth and walks down to work. When she gets to work, she is greeting with a surprise visit from her district manager.

"Jennette, I have been several complaints that you have been drinking on the job."

"That's absurd, I don't even drink."

"Well, you smell like alcohol now."

"I don't know how."

"Either way, I have no choice but to let you go."

"I can't believe this, I need this job, I am being fired for something I not doing. I am going to sue this place."

"That is your choice, but you need to turn in your keys and leave the restaurant."

Jennette leaves and heads straight back to the bottle. Jennette's new full time job, and her only friend, is the bottle under her sink at home. While Jennette continues to drink more heavily, Zander is the one that suffers at home.

Zander also is getting more and more distant at school every day. Even though school is a safe haven, he is afraid to tell anybody about what is going on at home, and it is getting worse every day.

Pretty soon, Zander is keeping to himself at all times. He eats breakfast and lunch by himself. He sits at recess and does not play with anyone. He doesn't respond to Ms. Miller, and it is really starting to show in his grades.

Zander actually makes it through his first year of school despite his struggles at home. He gets remedial instruction at school and actually despite being a shell of the boy that he was when he first started school, Zander actually has done enough to move on to the first grade.

8 DODGEBALL

First grade begins just as kindergarten ends. The entire summer has been an absolute nightmare. Jennette did find a new job, which turned out to be a better on than the one she was fired from. Zander still has no escape from the harsh reality he faces every day. Zander has even further isolated himself from everyone at school.

When school starts, it is still pretty warm outside, and the school has no air conditioning. Almost all of the students in the school are wearing shorts and t-shirts, but Zander is wearing pants and a long sleeved shirt.

But even worse about first grade is that now he has a gym class twice a week. Today is Tuesday, the first day.

Mrs. Phillips is a twenty year veteran gym teacher in the school, and has been appointed to develop a program for kids to have a more active lifestyle. She remembers the days of playing outside all day long with friends every day until the street lights would go on. Even then it would take a yell from the door from her mother to finally convince her to come inside for the night. Now these days are about social media, posting pictures, making videos and mp3s.

After lunch, her first class walks in the gym where she is waiting. It is Miss Babcock's first grade class, including a very passive little boy by the name of Zander.

"Welcome class."

"Hello Mrs. Phillips," say the entire class except Zander.

"As part of my new get active program, I have decided that this school year we will have a competition between all of the first grade classes in the entire school district."

The children start clapping and cheering. Mrs. Phillips stands in front of them just staring and waiting for them to get quiet. The children get quiet when they realize she is waiting.

"We will use our gym time as a way to practice for the end of the year competition. The first month this year, we will be playing dodgeball."

The children start cheering again and once more Mrs. Phillips gives them "the stare" again, and they quiet down faster this time.

"Now that you are quiet, it is time to pick teams. Devin and Joshua will be captains."

One by one the children are being picked when it comes down to one last child.

"I guess I have to take you Zander, you are the last one left," says Joshua.

Zander takes a slow walk to his team and then he slowly walks on the right side of the gym. He immediately stands in the right corner of the gym away from everyone else.

The balls are placed in the middle of the gym at the line that separates the teams and waits for Mrs. Phillips.

"Go!"

All the kids go running trying to get a ball except for Zander, who remains standing in the same spot he went to before they started.

Zander stands there with a blank stare until he realizes that there is a ball coming straight at him.

"You're out Zander," yells Devin.

Zander walks of the court holding his arm crying.

"Don't be a wimp; it's only a dodgeball," says Joshua.

Zander just looks at him but does not say a word. He just stands on the side crying.

"Look at Zander everyone, what a crybaby!" yells Joshua.

"Oh did I give the poor baby a boo-boo?" says Devin.

"That will be enough of that," says Mrs. Phillips.

A few days have passed since Mrs. Phillips put an end to the comments a few children were saying to Zander. But, it is now Friday, and Miss Babcock's class is back again for gym class and another day of dodgeball.

"Before we start today, I want to let the entire class know how disappointed I was with what went on Tuesday. Part of being active in the competition, all students in this class must show positive active sportsmanship as well, or you will not be able to be in the year end competition."

Mrs. Phillips decides to keep the same teams from Tuesday to allow more time for the children to play. Zander, of course, heads back to the same right corner. But as he stands there he does not realize the Mrs. Phillips said go and looks up just in time to see not one ball coming at him but four balls all heading straight at him.

The first ball bounces past him, but the other three are another story. The first one hits Zander in the leg, the second one hits Zander in the arm, and the third one hits him in the stomach.

Zander is the first one out, but this time he tries to hold back his tears, but a few tears trickle out. He stands on the sideline almost relieved that he is out and that he will not get hit again when all of the sudden…..

"Joshua caught the ball; Zander, you are back in." says Mrs. Phillips.

Zander slowly walks back onto the court to head back to the right hand corner, but he doesn't notice that there is another ball coming right at him. He looks up just in time to see the ball hit him right in the face.

"Zander are you okay," asks Mrs. Phillips.

Zander lies on the ground, but this time he is balling his eyes out. After a few moments, he gets up and walks off of the court.

"Zander, talk to me,"

"I'm fine, but I don't want to play anymore."

"Okay Zander, if you don't want to play anymore, I will find something else for you to do."

"Like what?"

"I need to keep you active, so what would you want to do."

"I like running."

"Okay Zander, we have two more weeks of dodgeball, but I will let you run around the track as the others are playing dodgeball. But, you will need to participate in the other stuff we do the rest of the year."

"Okay, I will."

"And I promise you that nothing we do the rest of the year will have anything being thrown and you."

The next two weeks Zander just runs around the gym during class, but keeping a watchful eye on the balls that are being thrown around him.

Dodgeball ends and Mrs. Phillips starts on the next activity; basketball.

"This is better, instead on the balls being thrown at me, they are gonna be thrown at a circle with a bunch of strings on it," Zander says under his breath.

Mrs. Phillips, in Zander's mind, solves the problem, but the problems for Zander are about to get worse, especially at recess.

As usual, Zander sits under a tree at the playground just watching others play. Most of the time it is just because how sad he feels inside, but sometimes it is because he in just in too much pain….and he does not want anyone to know.

When he sits under the tree by himself, usually no one ever bothers him. But this day is different. Joshua and Devin take a break from shooting hoops and heads toward Zander.

"Look at Zander, he is such a baby," says Joshua.

"Yeah," says Devin, "what a baby."

"Leave me alone," cries Zander.

"The baby is starting to cry," says Joshua.

"I am not a baby."

"Does the baby need his diaper changed?" jokes Devin.

"Why are you picking on me?"

"Why are you so wimpy that you can't play dodgeball?" asks Devin

"Yeah, you cry every time the ball touches you," adds Joshua.

"But it hurts."

"No, it doesn't, stupid," says Devin "does the baby need a bottle?"

"Stop picking on me!"

"We made up a song just for you, baby," says Devin."

"Yeah, do you want to hear it?" asks Joshua.

"I said leave me alone!"

"No, we won't, just sit there and listen to the song. Hear it goes," says Devin.

Devin and Joshua start singing together:

Baby Zander in the sky!
Gets hit in the arm and makes him cry!
When the ball comes near his face!
Tears start to fall down all over the place!

Pretty soon other kids on the playground are joining in. Zander is crying while others are laughing at him. He tries to hide his face in his lap to hide the tears, but that just makes the kids on the playground make fun of him more.

Zander gets up hiding his face, trying to walk away but the kids keep making fun of him. He pushes his way through the kids and finally breaks free from the crowd."

"Hey baby," yells Devin.

Zander turns around, and BAM! Devin hits Zander in the face with the basketball. Zander falls to the ground.

"Mommy, stop hitting me, it hurts!"

All of the kids just pause, not knowing why he said what he did. Until one voice is heard.

"Look everybody, Zander is crying for his mommy," jokes Devin.

Laughter is heard from all sides until they notice that Zander has a bloody nose. All of the kids scatter, afraid that they might get in trouble because Zander is bleeding. During all of the commotion, Jessica, the recess aide, comes over and sees Zander sitting on the ground with blood on his face and shirt.

"Young man, are you okay?"

"Yes, I am okay."

"But you are bleeding. How did that happen?"

"I got hit with the basketball."

"Okay, I will take you to the nurse, and she will get you all cleaned up before going back to class."

The recess aide walks Zander down to the Mrs. Sherman's office, the school nurse, which is sitting at her desk."

"What happened?"

"This little boy got hit with the basketball."

Okay, thanks Jessica, I will take it from here."

Mrs. Sherman gets Zander's nose to stop bleeding.

"Now level with me, Zander. Did you really get hit with a basketball?"

"Yes, why do you ask?"

"If someone did this to you, you can tell me."

"The basketball hit me in the face."

"Was it while you were playing on did someone throw it at you?"

"It just hit me."

"Okay, but I cannot send you back to class with blood all over your shirt."

"It's the only shirt I have"

"That's okay Zander; I keep extra shirts here just in case something like this happens."

Mrs. Sherman opens the door to the closet where she keeps the extra shirts. The shirts are all brand new, with the tags still on them.

"Today is you lucky day, Zander. You get to choose whatever color you want."

Zander looks at all of the new shirts. He starts to get a little nervous because he remembers the last time he was bought a new t-shirt. Zander begins to cry a little while thinking about his elephant t-shirt that his mother bought him from the zoo.

"Are you giving me a new shirt?"

"Yes I am, and you get to keep it."

Zander takes a moment and looks at all of the colors of shirts in the closet.

"Can I have a purple shirt? I never had a purple shirt before."

"A purple shirt it is."

Not thinking Zander takes off his shirt so he can put his new purple shirt on but forgets that Mrs. Sherman in sitting right in front of him……..and now she is sitting there with a confused but concerned look on her face.

9 SUSPECTED

"Do you have anything to tell me Zander?"

"No. Why?"

"You have bruises up and down both of your arms."

"I was riding my bike really fast, and I fell because I turned way too fast."

"But there are no cuts on your arms, just bruises."

"The cuts are gone. All I have is the dark spots now. They will go away."

"Okay, just be more careful when you ride your bike."

"Can I go back to class now?"

"Yes, go ahead."

Zander leaves Mrs. Sherman's office and heads back to class. The rest of the day finishes uneventful until after school.

Miss Babcock is sitting at her desk reviewing her lesson plans for the following day when Mrs. Sherman walks in.

"Do you have a minute, Miss Babcock?"

"How may I help you?"

"I was hoping I could have a minute to talk to you about what happened with Zander today."

"What exactly happened with him today?"

"He came to my office with a bloody nose. When I talked to him about it, I just got a strange vibe that he was hiding the truth from me."

"What gave you that strange vibe?"

"First, he seemed particularly reluctant talking about what happened. Then, when I gave him a new shirt because his shirt had blood on it, I saw bruises all over both of his arms."

"What did he say?"

"He said he fell off his bike."

"What do you think?"

"His injuries are not consistent with a child wiping out on his bike."

"So you think something else is going on?"

"I truly do."

"Maybe we should talk to Principal Gayle about this."

"That might be a good idea, when do you want to do it?"

"How about right now?"

"Okay, let's go."

Miss Babcock and Mrs. Sherman walk down to Principal Gayle's office.

"Principal Gayle, can we have a minute of your time?" asks Miss Babcock.

"No, you may not, this is my time. If you want to talk to me, it has to be before school or during your free period."

"But this is important."

"Not as important as my couch and television right now."

"But this really cannot wait."

"Well, it has to wait, I'm leaving right now. Goodbye."

Principal Gayle leaves Miss Babcock and Mrs. Sherman just standing there in disbelief.

"I cannot believe she would not make time for us."

"I know you are a first year teacher, but between you and me, and off the record, she stabbed a lot of people in the back to get to where she is right now.

All she cares about is herself and furthering her own career."

"No offense, Principal Gayle was a teacher and now a principal; there is no way she could be like that."

"Believe it; she also calls students into her office daily in order to collect dirt on the teachers in case she needs it."

"That's preposterous; I can't see anyone doing that."

"Give it time and you'll see what I am talking about."

The next morning both Miss Babcock and Mrs. Sherman arrive at the school early to talk to Principal Gayle.

"Do you have time for us now?"

"Really, I have all of this paperwork to get done, and I cannot get it done if I keep getting bothered by teachers that cannot do things on their own without me."

"This is important," adds Mrs. Sherman.

"Nothing you can say can be as important as my job right now"

"Maybe we will just take this to the superintendent instead," adds Miss Babcock.

"Fine, but you only have a minute."

"We are concerned about Zander; we think he might be getting abused at home."

"What makes you think that?"

"He has bruises on his arms that do not seem consistent with what he is saying."

"That really doesn't warrant our attention."

"How can you say that?"

"Mrs. Sherman, can you give me a minute alone with Miss Babcock."

Mrs. Sherman leaves and shuts the door behind her.

"Miss Babcock, you don't know enough about teaching to know what is going on….and don't ever question me in front of another adult in this school."

"Just because I am a first year teacher, it does not mean I am clueless to what is going on."

"That statement alone shows that you are clueless. You think that Zander is being abused. I don't believe you."

"But….."

"There is no but. Your role as a teacher is to get the students through to the next grade. Now that state standardized testing begins in first grade now, that is your focus in everything you do."

"So what you are saying is I should not teach the students, rather just take the year and prepare them for the test, nothing else."

"I cannot say that, but I am saying that."

"So how is Zander in any sort of way able to pass a test if this is possibly going on at home?"

"Leave that to me, he will make it through."

"So you are asking me to ignore this. That seems idiotic to me."

"Again, I am saying that it doesn't warrant our attention."

"How is Zander going to be able to function at all this year if this is going on?"

"That comes down to classroom management. If that is a problem for you; maybe teaching is not the right profession for you. Good day to you."

Miss Babcock leaves Principal Gayle's office in disgust. She stops by Mrs. Sherman's office on the way to her classroom.

"Now I see what you were talking about last night."

"I told you so."

The day goes smoothly because Miss Babcock is an excellent first year teacher, despite the lack of faith she received earlier from Principal Gayle. She was able to put the stress of that situation behind her so she could have a great day.

Miss Babcock decides instead of staying at school longer at the end of the day, she is going to take her work home with her. But, that is soon interrupted by Principal Gayle.

"Miss Babcock, about earlier, I want you to understand that even though I can't fire you because of your contract, the thought did cross my mine."

"You thought of firing me for sticking up for a student; trying to protect him."

"You called me an idiot."

"I never called you an idiot, I just said that is seems idiotic to ignore a child in trouble."

"That's just semantics."

"Semantics or not, I am going to do the right thing."

"I am going to tell you this and end this conversation; if you try to pursue this I will guarantee that you will regret it. I have the power to make sure your contract will not be renewed. Also, I have friends in high places in other schools, and I can make it so you never get a job in another district either. I also can get your teaching license revoked. So try me."

Miss Babcock does not say another word, and just stares at Principal Gayle as she walks out of her classroom. Despite her disapproval of the situation,

Miss Babcock respects the decision so she can prepare her students for the state tests.

The standardized tests week comes and goes, but the entire year, Miss Babcock, despite the objections of Principal Gayle, has been observing and documenting Zander's behavior and well-being daily.

The weekend after the tests, Miss Babcock is sitting in her apartment grading papers when she realizes she forgot her grade book at school. She decides to make a quick trip back to the school.

When she pulls into the parking lot, she sees Principal Gayle sitting in her office doing work.

"That seems strange that she is here on the weekend," Miss Babcock thinks to herself.

Principal Gayle did not even notice anyone walk into the school. But what Miss Babcock observes next will forever change her career. She sees Principal Gayle changing answers on the students' standardized tests.

"I cannot believe she is fixing the students' tests," Miss Babcock says to herself as she is walking out. "Luckily she didn't see me, because if she saw me see her changing answers, that would be the end of me at this school."

The next Monday, Miss Babcock has an early visitor in her classroom. It is Principal Gayle.

"Miss Babcock, I just found out from the superintendent that your position will be cut and that as of June first, you will no longer be employed by the school district."

"I expected that much; luckily I secured a job for next year already."

"You don't have to lie to me, just leave graciously without conflict when your contract is over."

Now that Miss Babcock has nothing to lose since she already has been informed of her situation, she decides to do one thing before the end of the school year.

"It is time to call Zander's mom in for a meeting."

The next day after school, Jennette shows up to meet with Miss Babcock.

"Hello, I am Zander's teacher. I just want to tell you it has been a privilege having Zander in my class this year."

"That is good to hear."

"But, I do have some concerns also."

"Concerns?"

"Yes, Zander tends to keep to himself almost all of the time, and he is highly passive in class."

"Zander is just a real shy boy; he doesn't even talk much at home."

"Even though I see that being a problem, his quiet demeanor is not why I asked you here today."

"Then why did you ask me here?"

"I am concerned about some of the bruises he has shown me this year."

"Zander can be such a clumsy kid sometimes, he is always running. He likes to try to run up and down the stairs at home and sometimes he falls."

"Are you sure that is what is happening?"

"What are you accusing me of? I love my son, and he just isn't as coordinated as other children."

"The way he acts in class and the bruises he shows me leads me to believe that someone is hurting him intentionally."

"I am not abusing my son and how dare you accuse me of doing that. I am insulted."

"I apologize, but I did not say I thought it was you, I am just saying that maybe this needs to be addressed. Maybe a neighbor or a babysitter is doing it."

"If it is happening, I am not the one doing it. He just needs to get out more and exercise. He needs to get stronger and not be so clumsy all of the time."

"My advice is to take him on bike rides. That is a great way to strengthen up his legs so when he runs, he won't fall as much."

"I am sorry, but I am a single mom, and do not make a lot of money. I cannot afford to buy him a bike."

"You're telling me he doesn't have a bike?"

"I wish he did, he would like that very much."

"Okay, maybe check garage sales this summer, you usually can find bikes really cheap, if you don't mind a used one."

"Okay, I will. Is there anything else?"

"No, that will be it. Thank you for your time."

Jennette heads back home and straight back to the bottle.

"I can't believe I have another stupid bitch teacher accusing me of hurting that thing. Has the world gone completely mad?"

The next morning, Miss Babcock again is greeted again by Principal Gayle.

"I told you to let it go, but you chose to ignore me."

"What are you talking about?"

"I just received a call from Zander's mom. She told me you accused her of child abuse."

"I never accused her of anything; I just wanted her to know my concerns."

"What part of it doesn't warrant our attention didn't you understand?"

"Oh, I thought you said it didn't warrant your attention, I didn't think you meant it didn't warrant my attention also."

"There you go with the semantics again. I am not one of your students; you cannot play games with me."

"I am not playing games; I just want to do what is right."

"You do not know enough to do what is right; you think that college taught you everything, but you don't know anything without experience. Good day to you."

After the school day ends, Principal Gayle returns to Miss Babcock's classroom, but she has the other two first grade teachers with her.

"Miss Babcock, all year long I have gotten nothing but complaints from parents about you. I am constantly getting complaints from your students that they just do not want to be in you class."

"I highly doubt that is true."

"Also, you violated confidentiality on a number of occasions."

"Is this what this is really about?"

"Yes, and I am also tired of hearing how you bad mouth the other first grade teachers. You say they are your colleagues up front, but act like they are your enemies when they are not around. I cannot believe I allowed a teacher to stay here that stabs other teachers in the back."

"I have never and would never say anything about my fellow first grade teachers. I love working with them. They have been helpful and supportive all year long. I cannot believe you would try to deliberately sabotage my relationship with them."

"Either way, it would be in the best interest of the school that you take the rest of your personal days, and I will arrange a sub for the rest of the school year."

"That's fine, but for the record I find it pathetic that you would do something this spiteful just to get back at someone that took a stand."

"Insubordination is not taking a stand."

"If standing up for a student is insubordinate, then I am happy to be labeled it."

Principal Gayle and the other teachers leave. Miss Babcock starts cleaning out her desk. Principal Gayle walks back in.

"I told you not to cross me, have a nice life."

9 THE VISIT

Julie Babcock's first year teaching in her eyes was a great success despite the nightmare that she had to deal with at the hands of a vindictive principal. But, her time dealing with a certain student is far from over.

Principal Gayle expected her to create daily lessons plans for the last few days of school. Instead, she left a binder on her desk at the school labeled daily lesson plans, but all that is in the binder is blank pages.

Julie sits at home relaxing knowing that she has nowhere to go the following day. She takes a hot bath, and then starts dinner so it will be ready when her fiancé, Brandon comes home.

"Hello, honey, how was your day."

"It was great, except for the whole firing thing."

"Firing? You were fired? Don't you have a contract?"

"I was asked not to return. She hired a substitute for the rest of the year."

"What happened?"

"It's a long story."

"Well it will give us something to talk about over dinner."

Brandon and Julie eat dinner and talk about how Principal Gayle set her up to be fired.

"What exactly caused this whole situation?"

"Well, I think one of my students is being abused. I approached her about it, and she told me to ignore it."

"Really?"

"Yeah, but when I chose to do something about it, she had me fired. Are you mad?"

"I could never be mad at you for helping a child. I am so very proud of you."

"At least I am getting paid to sit at home, but……"

"But what?"

"I just wish I could have done more."

"Who says you can't? I can give Rob a call."

"Rob? Your best man?"

"Yes Rob, he works for Child Services. He might be able to help if you're up for it. But, you need to have some sort of proof."

"I think I do. I have been compiling a running record on him since I started suspecting it."

"That should be a good start."

Brandon leaves the dinner table to call Rob. He returns a few minutes later.

"He will meet with us for lunch tomorrow."

"That will be super. Even if I am not teaching at the school, I can still be there for Zander to do what's right."

A few weeks later, Jennette is disturbed from a nap on the couch by a knock at the door.

"Are you Jennette?"

"Yes, can I help you?"

"My name is Rob Lawson; I am a representative from Child Services. May we talk?"

"Talk? About what?"

"About what is going on with Zander?"

"There is nothing going on with Zander; he is fine."

"I am not saying otherwise, I just would like to come in to talk."

"No, you cannot come in."

"Why are you being so hostile?"

"I am not hostile, but there is no way you are coming in."

"I am a representative from Child Services; I can take your child away, no questions asked if you don't cooperate."

"I know you do not have the authority to do that. If you want to get through this door, you will have to get a warrant."

"I do not need a warrant to do my job."

"The Fourth Amendment of the US Constitution says you do. Please get off my property."

"Maybe Zander can just come out here so I can talk to him."

"You will not talk to him; I do not give you permission!"

Jennette slams the door on Rob.

"Well, she really did her homework on this situation. Something must be going on if she refuses to let me in. I need to find some way to talk to Zander without her around."

Summer passes, and Zander returns to school now as a second grader. But, he still has not changed for the better.

One morning early in the school year, Principal Gayle is interrupted from her paperwork by a person that is not on the school staff.

"Hello, my name is Rob Lawson; I am a representative from Child Services."

"Why is Child Services visiting me?"

"A former teacher has reported that there is a child in your school that is possibly getting abused at home."

"That's terrible, but I wish she would have come to me about it."

"According to her report, she tried to come to you; but you told her to ignore it."

"Miss Babcock was an extremely inefficient teacher, and she is just getting back at me because her contract wasn't renewed."

"That is kind of childish to say, don't you think?"

"Well if you knew Miss Babcock, you would understand why I said that."

"To be honest, I do know Miss Babcock; she just married my best friend."

"Um……………..well…………….you see……..."

"Don't waste your time trying to figure out what to say. Admit it; I busted you in a lie. I bet your foot tastes great about right now. But that is not why I am here."

"Then why are you here?"

"Zander's mom will not let me talk to him, so I am hoping to talk to him while he is at school."

"I do not see that as a problem. I will call him right down."

Principal Gayle calls Zander down to the office and allows Rob to take to him.

"My name is Rob. What is your name?"

"I'm Zander."

"Hi, Zander, I was wondering if you would like to talk."

"You are that man that came to my house."

"Yes, I did come to your house."

"My mommy said not to talk to you."

"Why did you mother say that?"

"She said you are trying to put me in jail for being bad."

"I would never put you in jail; I just want to help you."

"I don't need your help, please leave me alone."

"But, if you mother is hurting you, I can get her help."

"Mommy says she doesn't need help. She is going to school to be a psychologist. She says that she can help herself because her classes teach her that."

"Honestly Zander, people, even psychologists have problems, but it takes others to help them. No one can do that alone."

"My mommy can, she says she is really smart."

"Okay, if you don't want to tell me anything, I understand. Can I give you something?"

"What's that?"

"This is a magic card. Call the number on the card if you need someone to come over to keep you safe."

"My mommy says she will keep me safe."

Rob leaves extremely disappointed that Zander would not let him help.

"If I can't get into that house, or get Zander to tell me what is going on, there is nothing I can do about it."

That night at home, Zander leaves his school book on the end table by the couch before he goes to his room for another night of cereal and solitude.

"You stupid little shit!" Zander hears from the other room.

"Get your ass out here!"

"Yes, mommy."

"What the hell is this?"

"That man came to see me today; he said that card is magic."

"Magic my ass!"

"Didn't you listen when I told you, stupid? This card is not magic; it is a ticket to a horrible place."

"That man was nice."

"That is a trick, he is nice and then he takes you to jail. Don't believe anything he says."

"But....but....mommy....he said he wants to help me."

"He does not want to help you; he wants to put you in jail. How dare you disobey me? Now, I am going to punish you like you have never been punished before."

At the end of the night, Zander lays in his room. He can barely move. His skin is not white anymore. He cannot even stand up to go to the bathroom.

The next morning is no different; he still is struggling to move around his room.

"Get up and go to school."

"I said, get up and go to school, stupid."

Jennette drags him out of the room and tries to stand him up. Zander immediately falls to the ground, holding his leg.

"Quick faking,"

Zander tries to get up on his own, but he falls down to the floor again holding his leg.

"Stupid little faker, fine, if you want to be like that. Go back to your room."

Zander tries to get back up, but he just does not have the strength. Instead, he slowly drags his limp body across the floor and finally makes it to his room.

"You should get an award for that acting job. Stay in your room, I am going out."

"Respond you stupid thing, you owe me that. I am your mother!"

"Okay, mommy."

Jennette leaves and heads straight to the school to confront Principal Gayle.

"I cannot believe you allowed someone to talk to my child without my permission."

"I don't need your permission; parents do not have any rights once their children walk through the door at school."

"You are telling me you can do and say whatever you want when it comes to my child."

"From nine to three, yes."

"How do they let such an idiot be in charge of a school?"

"That's your opinion."

"I want to know why you allowed someone from Child Services talk to my son."

"Oh, this is about Zander."

"Yes, this is what it is about."

"Well, I put a stop to it when I realized what was going on. You see, Rob Lawson is friends with one of Zander's former teacher. But she was very unprofessional, I had to fire her."

"Miss Babcock was fired?"

"I believe that she concocted a plan with Mr. Lawson is an attempt to get me in trouble. It had nothing to do with you."

"How can you say it has nothing to do with me?"

"Your son was just a pawn, used as a way to set me up."

"So you are telling me that Miss Babcock made this whole thing up?"

"Yes she did. But I didn't believe her."

"Okay, but you obviously do not have control of your school, so today is his last day at this school. I will homeschool him for now on. I do not play these childish games."

Jennette leaves after withdrawing Zander from the school. Principal Gayle sits in her office staring at Jennette through the window.

"It is a great thing that Zander withdrew. Now our test scores will be higher."

Jennette spends the rest of the school year with Zander at home. But, very little teaching is going on. The amount of physical and emotional abuse outweighs learning by a ratio of one hundred to one.

"I don't want this little thing around all of the time. He needs to go back to school. I can't live my life with him always around."

A couple of months later and before the start of the new school year, Jennette and Zander move to a new town, Portage, Indiana.

10 A NEW SCHOOL

Zander is now enrolled as a third grade student at Dunes Acres Elementary School. But before the school year starts, Jennette decides to have a meeting with the principal.

"Hello, and welcome to Dunes Acres Elementary School. I am Principal Taylor. How may I help you?"

"My name is Jennette, and I just moved to Portage and just enrolled my son in your school."

"Well, we are happy to have him here."

"But after the last school, I am a little weary of school because of the ailment that Zander has."

"I am happy to take the time to hear all about Zander."

"You see, Zander has been diagnosed with epilepsy if you know what that is."

"I know exactly what that is, what do we need to know so we can handle the situation properly?"

"Well, you see, Zander has violent seizures from time to time. He has medication that he needs to take twice a day. I give it to him in the morning and again at night so medication at school is not a problem."

"But, just in case we need to have a list of medication Zander takes for our file in the nurse's office, as a safety measure."

"Also, the medication also tends to make him….how do I describe this…….zone out from time to time."

"There is a lot of medication out there that causes that. One of our responsibilities as educators is to ensure that your child is able to focus in class."

"That is what I am hoping to talk to his teacher about."

"I would be happy to do that, but Zander is assigned to a class that the teacher just left to pursue other opportunities. I am in the process of hiring a new teacher."

"Okay, that is fine."

"But, once the new teacher is hired, we have two options; I can either set up a meeting, or I can just talk to whoever it will be about Zander's condition."

"I work like crazy hours, so I trust you to do the right thing."

"Thank you for your faith in me and in my staff, Zander will have a great year."

Jennette leaves reassured that her secret will be safe at this school.

"It is such a good feeling knowing that thing will be at a school where everybody is so naive."

A couple weeks later, it is time for Zander to go to his new school. He has mixed feeling about Dunes Acres Elementary.

"I am happy that I am going to a new school because I won't get made fun of, but I will be all alone with no friends again."

Zander gets off the bus on the first day of school and walks through the front door. He stands there looking around confused.

"Let me guess, you are new here."

"Yes, I am."

"Hello, I am Principal Taylor, welcome to our school."

"I'm, I'm Zander."

"Hello, Zander. Let me guess, you do not know where your classroom is."

"How did you know?"

"Just a wild guess, your classroom is down the hall, it is the first room on the right just passed the restrooms."

"Okay, thank you."

"If you need anything Zander, my door is always open."

Zander quietly and slowly heads down the hallway to his classroom with the same blank stare that he and everyone will soon be accustomed to.

"Zander?"

"Miss Babcock?"

"Yes, it's me, but it's Mrs. Lyons now."

"Mrs. Lyons?"

"I was married over the summer."

"Oh, am I in your class again?"

"Yes, is that a problem?"

"No, but mommy said you tried to get me in trouble last year with the police."

"I would never so that Zander. Trust me; this will be a great year for you. Let's go in and meet your new classmates."

Zander takes a seat at his desk and just sits there with a blank stare. All of the other students greet

Zander with open arms. Zander just give a smile and says nothing but his name.

A few moments later, the announcements start. Principal Taylor welcomes everybody.

"Welcome back students, teachers and staff to another glorious start of a new year here at Dunes Acres Elementary. This year's slogan for the school is 'It's Cool to Care.' This year, we are all going to care about each other and ourselves. Every year, we promote a positive school by making sure that bullying is not an acceptable part of how we should treat each other."

Zander begins to listen more attentively.

"This year will even be better. As a way of celebrating our no bullying in our school policy, every student with have the opportunity to earn "It's Cool to Care" tickets. Each student that earns one ticket every week of the year will be able to participate in an end of a year carnival and safety festival….right here at the school."

Cheers are heard all over the school.

"I will personally take time in every class to explain how to earn tickets. Have a super Dunes Acres day."

Mrs. Lyons introduces herself and begins an opening activity. Her desks are in groups, and there is a reason behind it.

"As a way to get to know each other, I have places items in a box for each group. There are paper plates, plastic cups, aluminum foils, some string, drinking straws, and a roll of tape. Work together and build a bridge."

One student asks, "How do we build it?"

"That is what your group will have to figure out."

Zander remembers this activity from last year, but he did not really participate. But, his group is struggling to get started.

Zander jumps in, "We need to take the plates and wrap them in foil; we can use the cups to hold the bridge up."

Pretty soon, the group is working together, bouncing ideas off of each other. The group is so into the bridge building that they did not notice that Principal Taylor is looking on as the work when Mrs. Lyons walks over.

"Mrs. Lyons, what are the kids doing?"

"They are getting a lesson on working together, and communication."

"Wow, this is a really neat idea. Do you mind that I sit in and observe."

"You are always welcome here, this is your school."

"Mrs. Lyons, I know you are new here, but this is our school, I am a guest in your classroom."

The kids finish building the bridges, followed by a group discussion on why it is so important to work together.

Then, Principal Taylor talks to the class.

"Good Morning everyone,"

"Good morning Principal Taylor," everyone says.

"This is what the tickets look like. Every adult in the school will have them. Your job is to earn them every week by being kind and helping others. When an adult see that, you will be awarded a ticket. But, there are fines, as well. Every time you are caught bullying, you will be fined five tickets. Finish the year with fifty tickets, and it will buy admission to the carnival."

Principal Taylor finishes talking about the tickets and starts to walk out of the class when she makes a brief pause.

"I noticed during the bridge building that one group started a little slow but finished great. One student in the class really helped his group get started, so I am going to award the very first ticket right now."

All the students stop and stare at Principal Taylor.

"This very first ticket goes to Zander, congratulations."

Zander walks up with a small smile on his face and gets his first ticket. Principal Taylor puts her hand out to shake his hand and Zander flinches.

"I am sorry, I did not mean to startle you, and I just want to shake your hand."

"Okay, thank you."

Later in the day during Mrs. Lyons' free period, Principal Taylor walks in again."

"I want to talk to you about Zander."

Mrs. Lyons nervously responds, "What about,"

"His condition."

"And what condition is that?"

"I had a meeting with his mother, and she told me about the epileptic seizures."

"Is that what she is saying now?"

"What?"

"Oh, nothing."

"You can tell me, I am here to support you."

"I had Zander in my class last year."

"Oh, so you already know about Zander."

"Yes I do, but thanks for giving me the heads up."

"You are very welcome; let me know if you need anything."

Principal Taylor leaves. Mrs. Lyons sits there thinking to herself.

"Do I really want to have a repeat of what went on last year? Do I want to be looking for a job again this time next year? I don't think I am going to tell her unless I know for a fact this time."

The last fifteen minutes in Mrs. Lyons class are used for silent reading. While the students are reading, she calls Zander to her desk.

"Zander, I will be truthful, I don't think your mom is going to let me be your teacher again."

"But I want you as my teacher."

"Okay, I will make a deal with you, I will make sure you get all of your tickets before the carnival, but never call me Miss Babcock at home. If your mom asks, my name is Mrs. Lyons. Can you keep it a secret?"

"Yes I will, I promise."

Mrs. Lyons heads home after school, but not before making a phone call.

"Rob, this is Julie."

"Hi Julie"

"You will not believe this."

"What's that?"

"Zander is in my class again….his mom moved him to a new school."

"Are you serious?"

"Yes, I'm serious. What should I do?"

"We failed this child last year, and we cannot fail him again. I just did not have enough evidence to prove anything. What I need you to do is document anything out of the ordinary, but this time it is between you and me."

"Okay, I will."

The phone call ends but not before Rob gives her instructions on how to document possible instances of abuse.

She creates a log sheet and keeps them in a file in her desk. The sheet includes

- Child's name, age, gender, address
- Parent's name and address
- Nature and extent of the injury or condition observed
- Prior injuries
- Actions taken
- Where the act occurred
- Reporter's contact information

Throughout the school year, Mrs. Lyons keeps thorough records of what she observes, especially because Zander is falling back into his old ways. But, one day she finally decides to make a phone call to Zander's mom.

"Is this Zander's mom?"

"Yes it is. What do you want?"

"This is Mrs. Lyons, Zander's teacher."

"That's great, what are you going to accuse me of this time?"

"I am not accusing you of anything, I am a new teacher and I am just trying to get a better understanding of his condition so I can be prepared in case something would happen."

"Oh, I am sorry, I just worked a long shift, and I am tired."

"That's okay. How often does he have seizures?"

"I would say he has them at least once a day."

"That's funny you say that."

"Why?"

"Because he never seems to have seizures at school."

"Are you accusing me of hurting my child?"

"No, I am not; I am just trying to help him"

"Well, I have rheumatoid arthritis and can barely lift my arms most of the time; so how would it be possible to hurt him?"

Jennette hangs up the phone on Mrs. Lyons; not realizing that Mrs. Lyons and Miss Babcock are the same person.

"That's funny, wouldn't her hands been kind of deformed in she has rheumatoid arthritis? I think I have enough for Rob to do his job."

11 SAVED

Jennette looks out the window of her new home in Portage and sees two cars in her driveway. One is a Portage police officer and the other car belongs to Rob Lawson.

After about a few minutes of ringing the doorbell, Jennette finally answers the door.

"I told you need to get a warrant if you want to come in."

"Do you mean a warrant like this?" says Rob.

The police officer hands Jennette the warrant and lets her know he is only there in case he is needed.

"I guess since you have a warrant, I guess you can come in."

"Jennette I am here to search your home. A few weeks ago, I received a complaint that Zander's basic needs are not being met."

"And who exactly complained?"

"I cannot divulge that information."

"You don't have to; I already know."

"So, where is Zander at?"

"He is visiting my mom in Hawthorne, Michigan right now."

"Okay, may I take a look around?"

"Go ahead, but you will not find anything."

Rob inspects the house and to his dismay, he cannot find any evidence that he can use against Jennette. She has plenty of food in the house, and Zander has his own room with a bed in it.

"I guess that will be it for now, but I will need to talk to Zander when he returns. I will call you to set up an appointment."

"Okay, have a nice day."

Rob leaves, completely disappointed that the evidence is not there to remove Zander.

Jennette watches out the window, waiting for Rob and the police officer leave. She immediately heads to the garage. She opens the trunk to her car.

"You stupid little thing. Who have you been talking to?"

"No one mommy."

"Don't lie to me," Jennette screams as she hits Zander in the face.

"I am telling the truth, please stop!"

"You don't know how to tell the truth, you are nothing and will always be nothing."

"I am not nothing."

Jennette grabs Zander by the hair, and drags him into the house and throws in his room.

"Since you cannot keep you stupid mouth shut, I guess you are done with that school."

"But I have enough tickets to go to the carnival. Miss Babcock I mean Mrs. Lyons told me so."

"Mrs. Lyons is Miss Babcock! Are you serious?"

"Miss Babcock got married, and she came to my school to teach."

"You have been lying to me this whole time. That is why that jerk Child Services guy came."

"I'm sorry, mommy!"

"You are such a bad kid, you are not going back to this school the rest of the year, and you will not go to the carnival."

Jennette beats Zander severely and leaves him alone in the house and heads to the bar around the corner.

A few days later, Jennette receives a phone call.

"Hello, this is Rob Lawson from Child Services."

"What do you want this time?"

"I am calling to set up the appointment to talk to Zander."

"Too late, he left to stay with my mom until the next school year."

"I see. Now I understand why Zander has not been at school lately."

"That's why. He has not had much time with her, and she is a special education teacher. I thought it would be a good thing if she could get him caught up and ready for the next school year."

"Okay, let me know if I can help."

"I think you helped enough already moron."

Jennette hangs up on Rob.

"Guess what you stupid little brat. No one knows you are here. No one is coming to save you."

Zander misses the last few weeks of school and then spends the entire summer locked in his room, with barely enough food to survive, but he does survive.

August comes, and the start of another school year is coming. Jennette is ready to have Zander out of the house again, but is very reluctant to send him back to Dunes Acres Elementary.

She heads to the school to register Zander. Upon leaving, she notices something that she has never seen before.

"Does that say Mr.?"

Jennette takes another look. Sure enough, Zander has a male teacher for the first time in his life.

"That is great; I won't have to deal with another pyscho woman this year. Male teachers are clueless."

About the third week of the fourth grade school year, Zander has his first writing assignment. The writing prompt focuses around the 9/11 tragedy. He has to write a one page paper on a person that is his hero, and why this person is his hero.

A week after Zander turns in his writing assignment, it is sitting on the desk of Principal Taylor. She makes a quick phone call."

"Hello, this is Principal Taylor from Dunes Acres Elementary School. Is this Rob Lawson?"

"Yes it is. How may I help you today?"

"I am looking at an essay from one or our students that I think you need to see."

"What is it about?"

"I think it is a cry for help?"

"Please say Zander wrote it."

"How did you know?"

"I will be right there."

Rob races to the school to meet with Principal Taylor. Rob immediately runs into her office.

"Let me see the letter."

"Okay, but level with me before I show you. How did you know this is about Zander?"

"Mrs. Lyons was Zander's teacher last year. She has suspected this and reported it to me." She actually lost her first teaching job for pursuing this."

"What type of person would fire a teacher for something like this?"

"I have asked myself that same question?"

"Why did she come to me about this?"

"She was afraid of going through what she went through the first time."

"I would never do that to a teacher, I have too much integrity."

"But, the problem is that despite everything Mrs. Lyons documented and all the investigating I have done, I still cannot prove anything; hopefully until now."

"I think you have the proof now, Rob. Read it,"

Rob grabs the letter from Principal Taylor. Before he starts to read it, he takes a huge breath.

"Are you okay Rob?"

"Yes, I just truly hope this is the proof that I need. I have been waiting a long time to save Zander."

Rob finally looks at the paper. It is title "My Hero" by Zander. He begins to read the paper to himself.

MY HERO by Zander

My name is Zander. I am in fourth grade. I do not have a hero because my teacher says a hero is someone that saves somebody else. I need to find a hero somewhere because I need saved. My mommy drinks way too much and when she does she yells a lot and hits me. She never makes me dinner. I only eat cereal. She used to give me baths that make me sick. The doctor says that bleach makes me sick so maybe she must have been washing me with bleach. I am never allowed out of my room. She beats me so hard sometimes that I can't walk. I cry so much. I remember one time when the doorbell rang at home; she grabbed me and locked me in the trunk of her car. She always says I am a bad boy, but I don't know what I did. So if there are any heroes left in the world, I need a hero....please send me a hero.

"I think you have the proof you need," says Principal Taylor.

"I hope so. But, I will need to set up a meeting a formal meeting with you and Zander's teacher to document everything that happened up to this letter showing up on your desk."

"That will be just fine."

"In a couple of weeks, I should have all the paperwork in order, and then we will meet so I can have you sign off on my reports and that should be enough to get Zander out of that home."

Two weeks later, early in the morning, Jennette hears the doorbell ring. Jennette answers to door to see Rob and two police officers.

"You better have a warrant; that is the only way you are getting in my home."

"Better than a warrant, I have a court order; I am here to remove Zander from this home."

"You can't do that. There is no reason to do that. I have done nothing wrong. I am not letting you take him."

"You can't stop me."

"That is why you brought the officers with…….because you need them to protect you."

"These officers are not here for me, they are here for you.

One of the officers opens the door and says, "Ma'am, I need you to step outside. You have the right to remain silent, anything you say can and will be used against you in a court of law…….."

The officers lead Jennette to the squad car, but she takes one last look. She notices Zander standing at the window looking at her. The officers place

Jennette in the car and drives away. Zander never sees her again.

Zander turns around from his window and notices someone standing in his doorway.

"Are you my hero?"

"No, I am just Rob."

"Are you here to save me?"

"Yes, Zander I am here to save you."

"My teacher says a hero is someone that saves someone else."

"Well, I guess I am your hero."

"Am I going to jail?"

"No, Zander, you are not."

"Where am I going?"

"You are going to live with a new family."

"Are they going to hurt me?"

"No one is ever going to hurt you again?"

"Do I need to bring anything?"

"You can bring anything you want. I have a bag here to pack up your clothes. If there is anything else you want, you need to grab it, and we need to leave in a few minutes."

Zander grabs a small box from his closet. It has a handful of zoo animals, an elephant t-shirt and a little stuffed elephant.

"Are you ready, Zander?"

"Yes I am."

Rob and Zander start walking out, but Zander stops.

"I forgot something."

"Okay Zander, I will wait for you."

Zander walks back into his room. He walks out with a handful of tickets in his hands.

"What's that?"

"These are tickets from Mrs. Lyons' class. They were for a carnival, but mommy didn't let me go."

"Why did Mrs. Lyons give those to you?"

"I earned them for being nice to people. Would you do me a favor? Can you give them back to her?"

"Why would you want to give them back to her?"

"She brought me a hero….she earned them."

"Okay, I will."

Zander says goodbye to the home and the hell he lived through for the very last time.

Later that night, Rob meets Julie and Brandon for dinner.

"Julie, I have a present for you. Close your eyes and hold out your hands."

Rob places the tickets in her hands. Julie opens her eyes.

"What are these for?"

"Zander asked me to give them to you. He said you earned them."

"What are you telling me?"

"I am telling you that it's over."

Julie looks down at the tickets as tears start to fall down her face.

"No, Rob, it's not over; it's just beginning.

12 THE AFTERMATH

Over the course of the next few years, Zander has shown improvement in every way. His grades are improving every year. He has made a lot of new friends at school. He even plays at recess. There are so many things he is doing for the first time in his life.

Zander has a new family also. Amy, his new mom and Noah, his new dad love him very much. They were never able to have their own kids, but they treat Zander as if he is their own.

Zander has been going to counseling ever since that special day; that he just calls "Heroes Day."

Zander has opened up to the horrors that he dealt with for the first ten years of his life. Every day, he thinks about his mother less and less.

Zander has his own room. In fact, he doesn't mind being in his room if he needs time to himself. He has his own computer, television and video game system.

One morning, Zander wakes early up to get ready for school.

"Good morning, son."

"Good morning new mom."

"Zander, you don't have to call me new mom."

"Sorry, force of habit."

"It's okay. Do you want some breakfast?"

"Sure, anything but cereal."

"When you are at counseling, address your fear of cereal," Amy says jokingly.

"I am not afraid; I just ate enough cereal to last a lifetime."

Noah walks into the room, "Where's my coffee, love?

"Right where it always is sweetie," says Amy.

"Oh God! Get a room," jokes Zander as he walks out.

"Have a great day," says Amy.

"I always do," says Zander.

Every day to Zander is so memorable the rest of his school years. By the time Zander reaches the age of eighteen, Zander has completely put his real mother and the abuse out of his mind.

"Are you ready?" Amy asks.

"Yes am I."

"Are you sure you want to do this Zander."

"As much I have grown to love the two of you over the past few years, I just know if my heart that this is the right thing to do."

"It is your choice Zander, we will respect you decision," adds Noah.

"Are you mad at me?"

"Zander, we could never be mad at you for doing what you feel is right. Either way, you will be our son."

The three of them leave to head to the courthouse for the adoption hearing.

Before finalizing the adoption, the judge asks Zander one last thing.

"Zander, I have never had a request like this. Are you sure this is what you want."

"Yes your honor, I really do."

"May I ask why?"

Zander pauses and thinks for a minute.

"I just have a feeling that I am going to need it in the future, but I cannot explain why?"

"Okay Zander, I respect your wishes, you are now legally adopted, but I grant you the right to keep your last name. Congratulations son and good luck."

Zander looks back and Amy and Noah and smiles. He now has a mom and dad that love him. The next few years of his life are the greatest.

One day early in his senior year, Zander comes home, and his mom and dad are waiting for him on the couch.

"Zander, this came for you today," Amy says.

'What is it?"

"It is a letter?"

"I know it is a letter, but who is it from?"

Amy hands Zander the letter.

"Oh, it's from the University of North Indiana."

"Open it."

Zander opens the letter and starts reading, "Congratulations, you have been accepted for the fall semester at the University of North Indiana."

"That is awesome, son," Noah says.

"I am so proud of you," says Amy.

"Thank you, I love you both."

"We love you too, Zander."

"So have you even thought about what you might want to do in college?" asks Noah.

Zander takes a moment, and for the first time in a long while, he thinks back to his childhood.

"I think I want to be a teacher if that is okay."

"Whatever you want we do with your life we support you one hundred per cent."

Before his senior year ends, and his future starts in college, Zander still has one more big night ahead of him…..prom.

Zander and his girlfriend, Stacy has been dating for almost three years. Zander wants the night to be perfect. He rents the perfect tuxedo, and even matches the color of his bow tie to Stacy's dress perfectly.

He rents a limousine for the night and makes reservations at the finest restaurant in town. His goal is making this night perfect for Stacy.

Zander rents a hotel room near the amusement park that they are going to after prom.

"Are you sure it is okay we spend the night together?" asks Zander.

"We love each other don't we?" asks Stacy.

"Yes we do"

Zander and Stacy are making out in the room, and things are starting to go a bit farther. Zander stops in his tracks.

"What's wrong, Zander?"

"Are you sure you want to do this?"

"Of course I do, I love you."

"I love you, too."

"But, you are not ready for this."

"I am ready, but can you give me a minute. I will be right back."

Zander walks out of the hotel room, leaving Stacy alone but confused. About five minutes later, Zander returns.

"Where did you go?"

"I had to get something."

"What?"

"A condom."

"You didn't have to."

"Yes I did, we are both heading to North Indiana, and I need to make sure we are responsible. I hope I didn't wreck the mood."

"There is no way you could ever wreck the mood, I love you too much. To be honest, I am happy you went for a condom, considering your past."

"My past is in the past."

"But it made you a stronger person. Now turn off the lights."

The next morning, Zander and Stacy are sitting in the hotel lobby eating breakfast.

"Stacy, I love you and I can see a real future with you."

"I feel the same way."

"But, I am a little scared about that."

"Why would you be scared?"

"What went on in my past makes me afraid because I don't want to turn out to be like my mother. I want children of my own someday, but I am really scared about that."

"You have nothing to be scared about; you will be a great father when the time comes."

"How do you know that?"

"Because what happened to you made you stronger, now use your past as a reminder of how you do not want to act. Anyway, I will be right by your side when the time comes."

Zander looks at Stacy with a confused look.

"Do you mean despite my past, you are thinking about being in my future?"

"I will be in your future as long as you want me to."

"Are we talking about marriage?"

Stacy returns the confused look.

"Zander, I am saying that in time when you are ready for the next step, don't be afraid to take it, I will be waiting, as long as it takes."

"What happens if I turn out like my mother?"

"You won't, I promise."

Zander takes Stacy home after an exciting day at the amusement park.

"Thanks for prom and everything else Stacy, I love you."

"I love you too, and thanks for being you."

Their relationship gets stronger and stronger through the entire summer. The day before the both of them are leaving for college, Zander invites Stacy's family over for a cookout. When everybody finishes eating, Zander stands up to make a speech.

"I am so happy that I am able to share this day with the people I care about. I went from an abusive home, and two people opened their home to me that now I am proud to call my mom and dad. Because of that, I became the person that I am today. It also brought me to the most beautiful young woman. I am so lucky to have her in my life, but Stacy I need you to come up here; I need to ask you something."

Stacy walks up and stands next to Zander.

"Stacy, you have been so understanding and supportive of me while I dealt with my past. You told me one day that when I am ready to take the next step, you would be waiting. That moment I knew I wanted to spend the rest of my life with you, so I wondering if you are still waiting for me right now."

"I told you I will always be waiting, I love you."

"Well, I want to let you know that I am taking the next step."

Zander gets down on one knee.

"Stacy, I love you and cannot envision being without you. Will you marry me?"

"Zander, I do not have to wait anymore; my answer is yes!"

The next morning the engaged couple leaves for North Indiana. Zander starts his education program while Stacy begins her nursing program. The two of them live in the same dorm but might as well be living in the same room freshman year.

After sophomore year, Zander and Stacy get married. They immediately move into housing for married couples on campus. Every day is like the first day they are married. Despite the hectic school schedules they both have, Zander and Stacy find time for each other.

Two years later, Amy and Noah, are sitting in an auditorium at the University of North Indiana campus waiting for their only son to graduate from college with a degree in elementary education.

The graduates walk into the auditorium, Zander notices his mom and dad sitting in the audience, and he smiles at him. He has a seat with his classmates and starts to reflect and thinks to himself.

"I cannot believe I am sitting here. I have a mom and dad that love me, and are here to support me. My beautiful wife is somewhere in this crowd of black gowns with a huge smile on her face. I survived something that most people cannot believe any child could possibly live through. In a million years, I would have never thought I would be sitting here waiting to get a college diploma."

Then he hears from a distance, "We are now going to acknowledge the graduates from the department of education."

Zander stands up with the rest of the education majors, and starts to walk toward the podium to get his diploma. He looks one more time at his mom and dad and smiles. He then looks at the crowd of black gowns and finds Stacy. She blows him a kiss. He catches it and touches his mouth. He looks down to wait for his name to be called and he starts to hear.

"Sandra Jenkins, Samantha Johnson, Debbie Kovak, Kaylie Lawson, George Lenburg, Vanessa Lyles, Zander………………………………….."

13 BACK TO REALITY

"Zander"
"Zander"
"Earth to Zander"
"Mr. Madison!"
"What?"
"Hello"
"Hello back to you."
"I came in to tell you there are snickerdoodles in the teachers' lounge. I know they are your favorite."
"Thank you, been there…done that."

"Are you alright?"

"Yes, I was just thinking."

"Thinking about your past?"

"How did you know?"

"Let's see, Rob Lawson meets with Principal Taylor, and a child is removed from an abusive home. Kind of sounds familiar doesn't it?"

"Yeah, it does."

"If you need to talk, I am here."

"Thank you."

"I will talk to you later."

"Wait Miss Babcock"

"Zander, you have not called me Miss Babcock since the second grade."

"Sorry, I meant Mrs. Lyons."

"We are colleagues now Zander. You can call me Julie."

"Okay Julie. Thank you…But I am wondering. When I was in your class, could you have ever imagined being here having this conversation right now."

"To be honest Zander, I thought you would be dead."

"Trust me; I actually thought the same thing."

"Take a walk down to my classroom; I want to show you something."

Julie and Zander walk down to her classroom. As they walk in, Zander notices a picture frame on the wall.

"Are those the tickets I gave back to you?"

"Yes, they have been in my classroom ever since you gave them back to me. But, I now want to give them back to you. You earned them."

Zander takes the tickets back to his classroom and immediately hangs them on his wall. He looks at them and smiles. Zander leaves the school for the day.

When he gets home, Stacy is waiting for him with dinner on the table.

"How did it go?"

"Do you remember how I celebrate Heroes Day?"

"Yes"

"Well, I get to share it with someone now."

"That is terrific news; you are such a great man."

"Thank you my love."

"Are you alright?"

"Yes, but I need to do something. Will you go with me?"

"Zander, I would walk the world with you, I love you."

"I love you too."

Zander and Stacy eat dinner and leave for the night. They have a long drive ahead of them. They stop at a hotel for the night.

The next morning, they arrive at the Indiana Prison for Women. Zander and Stacy are greeted by the guard at the door.

"Who are you here to see?"

"We are here to see Jennette Madison."

Zander and Stacy wait at a table for about fifteen minutes before a woman in a bright orange jumpsuit approaches them and sits down across from them. She appears to be completely beaten down by life.

"Who in the hell are you guys?"

"I know it has been a long time, but you are telling me that you do not recognize your own son?"

"Zander?"

"Yes, mom."

"Your lies ruined my life, it is hell in here. I cannot believe you did this to me?"

"You did this to yourself."

"You were nothing but a loser then, and you are probably a loser now."

Stacy jumps in, "You don't know what you are talking about, your son turned out to be a great man that I love dearly."

"You don't know what you are talking about bitch."

Zander jumps in, "Stacy, can you give me a moment alone with my mom?"

Stacy leaves Zander and Jennette alone.

"That is a fine piece of work you brought with you."

"I am not here to discuss her. I am here to discuss what's wrong with you."

"The only thing that is wrong with me is that some punk kid got me put in here!"

"One day mom, you are going to wake up and realize what you did all those years. But, that is still not why I am here."

"Oh please, please tell me why you are here?"

"A million times it has run through my mind what I would say to you if I ever see you again. But now that I am sitting here looking at you, all I can say is thank you."

"Thank you?"

"Yes mom, thank you. Thank you for beating me all those years. Thank you for making me feel so worthless. Thank you for not loving me."

"Wow, you still are a stupid little thing."

"No mom, I am not. Because of you, I have the greatest parents in the world. Because of you I have the greatest wife in the world. Because of you I have saved another child from a person like you. I am a teacher now, and just like the teacher that saved me, I knew how to save him because of what you put me through."

"Oh, that stupid teacher, how is that useless pyscho Miss Babcock?"

"Her name is Julie, and I teach at the same school as her. She is my friend."

"You just don't get it Zander. I had a life before you. That life was taken away from me because of you."

"You know mom, one day you are going to wake up and realize what you have done, and hopefully you will have the courage to make yourself better.

Maybe then, and only then, you will take responsibility for your actions."

"You do not know what it was like to raise you, Zander, you probably don't have kids. You don't know what I know."

"Well I know one thing. I know that when I lived with you, I had to sleep with one eye open. I know now I can finally close both eyes because I am no longer afraid to see what is there when I open them."

"Well, that is just stupid. I am getting out of here soon, and I will finally get to live the life you stole from me."

"Do you know when you finally get out of here, and you make the next step in your life?"

"What about it, Zander."

"I will not be there waiting for you."

Zander walks away leaving Jennette sitting at the table. This is the last time he sees his real mother again. Zander walks to his car where Stacy is waiting.

"I am so sorry I yelled at your mom."

"Don't be, she deserved it."

"So, what now?"

"Now it's over."

Zander and Stacy get into their car to start the long drive home.

"I am so proud of you Zander. You finally have made peace with your mom; and yourself."

"I know, but................"

"There is no but Zander, your life will always be your own, and it will be what you make of it. From this point on, your life will be better than it ever has been before, and part of the reason is that you get to spend it with me."

Zander smiles at Stacy, "But my mother said something before I left that made me start to wonder."

"What did she tell you?"

"She said I cannot understand her because I do not have kids."

"What does having your own kids have anything to do with what she put you through?"

"She says having me ruined her life. And it makes me a little scared about being a father."

"Zander, I love you, and I am going to spend forever with you. If I didn't feel someday you would make a great father, I would not be sitting here right now."

"You know what, you are right."

"Of course I'm right; I'm your better half."

"More like my best half. You know what, my name is Zander Madison, I am not and will never be my mom, and I am going to be a great father someday."

"I am so glad you said that."

"And why is that my love."

"Because there is something I need to tell you………………………………."

THE END……WELL, JUST THE BEGINNING

FROM THE AUTHOR

The characters and events in this story are fictional. But, there are children in this world that are looking for a hero, just as Zander was looking for one. It is imperative that all people, not just teachers, understand the signs that children display when there is abuse in their lives. As an educator, I look for ten signs in a child when identifying possible abuse as defined by Safe Horizon's Child Advocacy Center:

1. *Unexplained injuries.* Abused children display burns, cuts and bruises, possible in a shape of a certain object. Also, the explanations are unconvincing.
2. *Changes in behavior.* Abused children tend to be depressed, scared, anxious and withdrawn. Sometimes, they are more aggressive.
3. *Returning to previous behavior.* Abused children may display behaviors from earlier years as bed wetting, thumb sucking, and fear of the dark or other adults.
4. *Fear of going home.* Abused children can be nervous about going home.

5. *Changes in eating.* Abused children may show weight gain or weight loss.
6. *Changes in sleeping.* Abused children have trouble falling asleep, and have nightmares. They also tend to be tired in school.
7. *Changes in school performance and attendance.* Abused children are absent from school a lot in an attempt to hide abuse. Abused children have difficulty concentrating in school.
8. *Lack of personal care of hygiene.* Abused children may have severe body odor, or dirty. They may also lack appropriate clothes for the weather.
9. *Risk-tasking behavior.* Abuse children may use drugs or alcohol. They may also carry weapons.
10. *Inappropriate sexual behavior.* Sexually abused children may display sexual behavior beyond their years.

If a child approaches you about being abuse, have the courage to report it. Teachers, doctors, and administrators are required by law to report abuse. Each state has its own guideline.

Remember if a child approaches you and says that they are being abused:
- Stay calm
- Believe the child
- Show interest and concern
- Reassure and support the child
- Report it to the state of local child protective services, or to the local police department.

There are things that you must not do also:
- Do not panic or overact
- Do not pressure the child
- Do not confront the offender
- Do not blame the child
- Do not overwhelm the abused child with questions

For more information and reporting abuse by state please visit the Child Welfare Information Gateway at:
https://www.childwelfare.gov/

No World around Me
by Dale S. Ailes

Where's the love?

Not here, no one to care for me.

Where's the warmth?

Not here, I am so cold.

Where's the support?

Not here, I am so all alone.

Where's the joy?

Not here, no one to make me laugh.

Where's the compassion?

Not here, I wish I had a friend.

Where's the fullness?

Not here, I am so empty inside.

Where's the pleasure?

Not here, all I feel is pain.

Where's the help?

Not here, no one to look my way.

Where's the savior?

Right here, teaching me today!

ABOUT THE AUTHOR

Dale S. Ailes is a licensed educator in the state of Indiana. He currently resides in Portage, Indiana with his wife, Amy and his daughter, Taylor. Dale received his Bachelors of Arts in Education from Purdue University North Central in 2009. He is currently pursuing a master's degree in higher education and learning. His goal is to educate a future generation of teachers about the roles and responsibilities of reporting potential cases of child abuse.